THE PRIVATE FUTURE

Books by Martin Pawley

Architecture versus Housing
The Private Future

THE PRIVATE FUTURE

Causes and Consequences
of Community Collapse
in the West

MARTIN PAWLEY

RANDOM HOUSE NEW YORK

All rights reserved under International and Pan-American Copyright
Conventions. Published in the United States by Random House, Inc.,
New York, and simultaneously in Canada by Random House of Canada
Limited, Toronto. Originally published in Great Britain
by Thames and Hudson Ltd., London.

Library of Congress Cataloging in Publication Data
Pawley, Martin.
  The private future: causes and consequences of
community collapse in the West.

  Includes bibliographical references.
  1. Civilization, Modern—1950-   2. Regression
(Civilization) I. Title.
CB428.P4   901.94   73-5044
ISBN 0-394-48072-4

Manufactured in the United States of America
First American Edition

For my wife, Clare

CONTENTS

INTRODUCTION

On a clear day any passenger flying in to one of the major cities of the Western world will see below him hundreds upon hundreds of separate houses extending into the distance and ringing the city to a depth of twenty or thirty miles. Similar houses string out along the highways and here and there expand to engulf the more tightly planned structure of an ancient town or village. Even in the centers of the cities these same structures penetrate, stacked up on end in the form of apartment blocks vying with hotels and offices of a similar general appearance. Everywhere these private enclosures are linked and interlaced by roads—from expressways to winding tracks—upon which run innumerable metal capsules, smaller, faster, but equally discrete and equally endless in their distribution over the landscape. From Anchorage in Alaska to the suburbs of Cape Town, from Tokyo to the landlocked enclave of West Berlin the same pattern unfolds irrespective of climate, topography or language. This grand design, wrought with endless repetition from two elements, the private dwelling and the private car, is the pattern of community in the Western world, and the scale of its achievement is such that an equal distribution of population throughout the dwellings in any developed country would give every individual his own private room and still leave hundreds of thousands of rooms unused. A similar distribution in, say, Pakistan would result in each room holding nine people. In some developed countries, notably the United States, the entire population could be accommodated in private automobiles, none of them full. In India the same distribution would result in more than one hundred persons crowding around each car.

This massive allocation of static and mobile private space is the most obvious difference between East and West. To a visitor it is the clearest demonstration of his entry into a different world; a world in which the terms "community," "family" and "society" have meanings so utterly different from those to which he has become accustomed that he may often wonder at their retention in the languages of the countries he visits. Those three words, it must seem to a visitor from Pakistan or India, cannot apply in any intelligible sense to the life he sees going on around him; they are but a camouflage and a pretense, a quaint verbal system for discussing the logistics of a population of anonymous consumers who long ago abandoned territoriality in the sense of entailed inheritance, and community in the sense of a delicate hierarchy of rank. Standing among the hundreds of cars parked at any suburban railway station, our visitor must begin to question this anomaly. Can these shoals of anonymous commuters fed on sports reports and salacious advertising really be called *communities?* Are these thinly populated, fenced-off brick boxes really the homes of *families?* Do ten or twenty million of them amount to a *society?* Surely not: there must be other words to use.

In the private world of the West the chain mail of the old social contract has rusted away, and overlaid upon it is a new, linear pattern of supply and consumption which has erased all intermediate regimes. There is now nothing but a vacant, terrorized space between the government—which controls and maintains production—and the isolated consumer, who increases his consumption in proportion to his isolation. Public life today is the glimpse of the celebrity linked with the product. No one knows his place any more, only what he wants. Newspapers, books, magazines, television programs catalogue the collapse of neglected edifices in the huge wasteland left by the old system of obligations and duties that once monitored social behavior even as they equivocally present new systems, new economies, new methods of providing more from less. The peoples of the West have subtly become gamblers, habituated to trading twenty per cent wage increases against sixteen per cent inflation to show a four per cent gain in wealth before moving on to new tables. Surely the old words cannot adequately describe this paradoxical, acquisitive transience.

Apparently they can, for our Asian visitor will soon discover that far from falling into obsolescence, the old words today possess a heightened, almost charismatic power. Shall we join the Common Market? Let the *community* decide. Do we wish the return of capital punishment? Let us ask the *community*. Can we permit abortion on demand? The *community* must answer. In every case the operative word is the pronoun of the first person plural, the word "we." "We" has become the symbol of community, yet when we use the word "we" we really mean "I." The questions mean do *you* want it, and the answer is always a deflection, don't ask *me,* ask *them*. Thus when a politician announces that "we" must curb our wage demands in order to combat inflation, the fact that he does not include himself in the exhortation is obscured rather than betrayed by the fraudulent "we." Both the cajolery and the anticipated response originate out there, somewhere among them, the *community*.

The word "family" occupies the same powerful but ironically

shifting ground. Scanning newspapers, our visitor notes the demand for "family entertainment"—though nowhere does he see evidence of the need for it. He hears talk of "family budgets," "family holidays," "the family doctor"—although most medical practices are drifting into anonymous clinics. He sees "family cars" which can do 100 mph, hears "family jokes" —which are not funny—and "family favorites"—which apparently no one buys. He sees "family encyclopedias" which nobody ever consults. Family life, he is assured by politicians displaying their own grinning offspring, lies at the foundation of community. And community itself is but an affectionate diminutive for *society,* a similar abstraction existing largely in a world of reassuring phrases. "The Great Society," "The New Society," "the open society," "the closed society," "the acquisitive society," "the affluent society"; or more darkly, "the responsibility of society"—a responsibility nobody wants to accept. Even the most absurd and oxymoronic political rantings: "The nation is a family,"[1] The community is society," turn out to be no less acceptable than the mysterious "Marlon Brando *is* the Godfather."

"Without traditions," observed a character in a recently successful musical, "our lives would be as shaky as a fiddler on a roof." Without illusions, our visitor might paraphrase, the fabric of mutual responsibility in the West would be swept away and black waves of anarchy (in the journalistic sense) engulf us all. By a tradition that has become an illusion the people of the West believe that unless each individual allows himself to be defined by his family, his community, and ultimately his society, the system of order that preserves social equilibrium in the face of inequality will dissolve overnight. Every crime statistic, every drug arrest, every campus disturbance, every day of production lost through industrial action is presented by the mass media in the context of just such a

---

[1] Harold Wilson in the House of Commons, November 20, 1972.

threat. The idea of a general public good remains a key element in the *mythology* of all Western societies, even though its status in reality has declined to a level where more and more stringent law enforcement is thought to be necessary to bring it to the notice of increasingly irresponsible citizens. Today, when an individual survives in proportion to his ability to *abandon* the traditional ties of family, community and society, he still listens politely to a strident rhetoric of law and order, restraint, discipline and good citizenship and detects no paradox. Such contradictions are only clear to those who visit from an older, more interdependent and smaller world. Almost drowned by the obsolete language of a paternalistic, maternalistic and patriotic past, the Western actor reads the lines of old plays while acting out new ones. His new privatized, isolated yet strangely Dionysian world is emerging into a deathly silence. Only mourners attend the birth of the anti-social society of the future, mourners who denounce every fetus as an irresponsibility, every child as a potential delinquent.

The use of such terms as "alienation" and "lowered social capacity," even the phrase "counter-culture" itself, conveys a clear impression of the supposed *illegitimacy* of the individual who renounces the old system of obligations. Like the pretense that the Nazi regime in Germany was an inexplicable throwback to barbarism with no roots or consequences in Western Europe, the idea that the emerging society of privatized, uninvolved, anti-community individuals is somehow *divorced* from its parentage, offers a perverse comfort to those who cannot see the extent to which their own lives are made up of the same tendencies.

In our addiction to antiquated terms like "community" we display an inappropriateness of vocabulary that prevents us from understanding what is happening before our very eyes. The flight to the suburbs away from village and urban community represents not so much the destruction of an ancient way of life as the logical development of tendencies implicit in the development of industry and—increasingly importantly—media. Just as ownership of a car, a vacuum cleaner, refrigerator, washing machine, radio and television reduces the need for dependent *social* contact, so does perfect contraception, an ideology of personal liberation, a set of stereo headphones, a joint or a needle reduce the need for dependent *personal* contact. The suburbs are not a fate, they are the incubators of a new world whose children merely extend the withdrawal of their parents by dropping out, abandoning the obsolete servitude of obligation altogether. Since the Industrial Revolution began, the Western world has witnessed the collapse of the idea of empire, and cracks appear between the minorities of the nation itself; the collapse of religion and the appearance of cracks in the individual psyche. The collapse of the extended family and the appearance of cracks in the nuclear family. The whole process of Western objective thought promises yet further fragmentation—factory farming, for example, employs only the processes of nutrition and reproduction in animals to the exclusion of the wholeness of their existence. Human beings drugged, hypnotized or tranquilized into a fantasy-laden nirvana approach the same extremes in their subdivision of the elements of consciousness.

Western society is on the brink of collapse—not into crime, violence, madness or redeeming revolution, as many would believe—but into withdrawal. Withdrawal from the whole system of values and obligations that has historically been the basis of public, community and family life. Western societies are collapsing not from an assault on their most cherished values, but from a voluntary, almost enthusiastic abandonment of them by people who are learning to live private lives of an unprecedented completeness with the aid of the momentum of a technology which is evolving more and more into a pattern of socially atomizing appliances.

If the collapse of community is in fact passionately desired, and consumer goods themselves are valued primarily as tools for social disengagement, then it follows that efforts to analyze this collapse as if it were a "disease" can never form the basis for an effective "cure." Thus when the Duke of Edinburgh lectures doctors[2] on the necessity of understanding the "physiology and psychology of new communities" before the "functioning and malfunctioning" of their individual members can be treated, he is not merely quoting from the administrative orthodoxy of our time, but also declaiming the limitations of its vision.

If the "diseases" of community can never be cured, neither can the innocent proposals frequently made by ecologists for the *voluntary* reduction of consumption in the interests of posterity or the third world ever bloodlessly triumph over the contrary demands of the consumer life-style. Affluence is essential to Western societies, not an optional extra: without it, or the hope of it, they no longer possess any basis for social harmony.

The decline of public life is both a result and a cause of privatization. A syndrome has been built up around the vacation of the public realm, its reoccupation by welfare bureaucracies, and the subsequent pattern of administrative terrorism that encourages a further exodus by those able to escape. Every year this cycle gains strength so that one by one the principal areas of public life, travel, communications, politics, sport and many others fall prey to security restrictions which endanger their very practicality. Air travel, for example, is made even more insufferable by the security precautions which guard against hijacking than it is by the fear of hijacking itself. Even the innocent world of correspondence is threatened not only by the prospect of letter bombing, but by the consequences of efforts to contain it.

Beyond the voluntary abandonment of social obligation and

---

[2] Address to the Royal College of Practitioners. Reported in the London *Times,* November 2, 1972.

community life, and beyond the corresponding uninhabitability of what is left of a public realm dominated by bureaucracy and crime, there is a pattern of private withdrawal which is as obscure in its psychology as it is apparently transparent in its external shape. This is something I have termed secondary reality—a kind of willful self-deception about the nature of events which is adopted as a survival strategy at all levels of society. In government policy it is expressed in the tortured logic of attempts to justify the protection of Western interests against a morality which holds, by and large, that they are indefensible. At the level of individual survival it is reflected in the matter-of-fact acceptance of the fantasies and deceptions of advertising, and the delusions of status that entertainment media cultivate in the private citizen. Secondary reality is dependent on media, and with the decentralization of media it will itself decentralize into myriad fantasies sustained by cassette video and Polaroid cameras, complex sound systems and refined drug experiences. I have traced the origins of this phenomenon back to the absorption of surrealism and psychoanalysis by the commercial art of advertising and marketing, and attempted to explain its mode of operation by reference to the mechanism of visual deception inherent in reliance upon recording media. Whether secondary reality really is a unitary phenomenon, or merely the sum of a number of different and perhaps altogether simpler aspects of media distortion may be a matter of doubt. I am mindful of the dangers inherent in the creation of neologisms of this kind, but a conviction that something is emerging through media which is changing the very basis of truth via the process of perception itself, grew in the course of writing this book.

Faringdon, England
December 1972

CHAPTER ONE

COMMUNITY ...
FAMILY ...
SOCIETY

SAN LEANDRO, CALIF., Feb. 17 (UPI)—The body of a victim of a hit-and-run accident lay three days just a few feet from his damaged car beside a busy freeway here. The body of Gary S. Voorhies, a 25 year old University of California student, was found Tuesday beside the Nimitz Freeway by a friend who had spotted his parked car on the freeway shoulder, the police reported.

The New York Times, February 2, 1973

According to the *Shorter Oxford English Dictionary* the word "community" has two basic meanings: the first is "the quality appertaining to all in common," and the second is "a body of people organized into a political, municipal or social unity." The fourth subsidiary meaning in the common quality line is given as "society, the social state," and the example of usage, Steele's "Marriage is the foundation of community," which dates from 1712 and neatly links the already related terms "community" and "society" with the concept of the family. The word family itself derives from the two Latin words *familia* (household), and *famulus* (servant). As a definition the same dictionary offers "members of a household, parents, children and servants," thereby embodying another central notion, the idea of inequality in rank. The word "society," notwithstanding its emergence under the heading of community, is itself defined as "a system or mode of life adopted by a body of individuals for the purpose of harmonious coexistence." It derives from the Latin *socius,* meaning companion or ally, and in concise dictionaries is often fused with the meaning of community in such definitions as "society: any social community." The generic term "social" yields definitions which encompass all three terms, for example: "Living in companies, gregarious, interdependent, existing only as a member of a compound organism." Here the central ideas of community, family and society achieve their clearest expression and reveal their conventional relationship: "society" is an organism consisting of "communities" which are interdependent and made up in turn of "families," which are the smallest accountable units of mutual obligation.

This then is the generally accepted meaning of terms whose interchangeability is seldom if ever scrutinized. The use of the term *community,* in particular, is almost a reflex among politicians and public figures of all kinds; priests, newspaper editorializers, columnists, popular moralists and law enforcement agencies, all find it a useful word. The community is the majority, it is legitimate public opinion—even when its most pronounced characteristic is silence. That this organization of concentric rings of obligation and responsibility extends back into history is evident from the ancient terms used to define it.

There is nothing new about community, it originates in those very conditions of scarcity, poverty and interdependence that obtained for the majority of the people of all nations until the very recent past. What is new is the bankruptcy of meaning that the term now possesses. The conditions of life have changed dramatically over the last thirty years for that very majority whose status as "the community" remains largely unquestioned today. So much so that to compare the definitions listed above with the reality of their late twentieth-century presence is simply to reveal glaring discrepancies. Let us begin with the smallest unit.

THE FAMILY

The family, defined in 1545 as "the body of persons who live in one house or under one head, including parents, children and servants," has shown a numerical decline ever since the gathering of reliable statistical information on the subject began over one hundred years ago. In 1861 the average number of persons per dwelling in England and Wales was over five, by 1966 it had sunk to under three, and this despite a doubling of the population during the same period. Parallelling this drop in household size, room occupancy itself has decreased in inverse proportion to overall dwelling size, which is to say that the smallest households now provide the largest amount of space per person. Increases in dwelling size, such as that recorded in Germany between 1952 and 1970, when the average area rose from 55 square meters to 75 square meters, are almost all accounted for by the space demands of increasing numbers of consumer durables which diminishing households require. Thus the disappearance of domestic servants, in 1861 present in over twenty per cent of the households in England and Wales, has been more than compensated for by the rapid incorporation of increasing numbers of inanimate energy slaves doing the same jobs.

To restore the classic definition of the family to full consonance with these realities means to incorporate into it fewer people and more machines: to leave the machines out, as is customary, is to present the family as a small group of survivors from the populous Victorian household seen against a backdrop of dumb commodities which have nonetheless steadily increased their dominance of the available space. This trend towards a lower rate of occupancy is generally interpreted as an indication of improved living standards, which in some senses it is. But in an altogether more fundamental way it reflects the fact that people today spend much more time at home than they used to. Increased space standards are as much a response to the increased demands which people make upon their homes, as they are to a notional demand for better standards of comfort and hygiene. The passing of the old pattern of community life, the decline of small-scale public entertainments, the closure of the bars, cafés, restaurants and clubs of small towns and villages, all reflect an unprecedented emphasis on the home as a place to *live* as opposed to a place to stay. Part of the depopulation of the crowded nineteenth-century dwelling is a response to the more exacting demands of persons who increasingly regard their homes as their *total environment*. The demand for private gardens reflects the same change.

If the absolute number of persons in the family has decreased, and one whole category disappeared altogether, so has the parallel notion of allegiance to "one head" suffered considerable change. In the modern nuclear family the string of dependent relatives for whom the head of the household accepts reponsibility has been drastically shortened, partly by the increased longevity of householders themselves, and partly also through the growth of social services designed to protect their independence to the grave. Grandparents, aunts, uncles and other peripheral figures no longer populate the family home—or indeed provide continuity between generations. On the contrary, their disappearance to retirement villages or institutions has simply foreshadowed the increasingly eager departure of the children themselves, not on the occasion of their marriage, as was formerly the case, but as soon after leaving school as possible. Even the wife, whose personalized service makes possible the pattern of male employment found in most affluent societies, shows signs of refusing to accept her lot for very much longer.

The high proportion of wives who work, as well as the growth of the responsibilities allowed to fall to the hands of extra-familial organizations such as schools and law enforcement agencies, threaten the status of the head of the household. Marriage itself, the key union in the formation of the household, is undercut by rising divorce statistics which, depending on the relative ages of husband and wife, can force from a quarter to a half of all conjugalities into separation.

Even the physical cradle of the family, the ancestral home, has largely retreated to the status of an image. On average every mortgage in Britain lasts seven years—which is to say that the average owner occupier moves house at the end of that time. In the United States the interval is shorter at five years, and a quarter of the American population moves house every year. In Washington, DC, of 885,000 subscribers listed in the phone book in 1969, over half were new entries. The moves themselves are not generally over short distances. At a time when the pressure of evolving commercial and industrial technique can make whole ranges of jobs obsolete in less than a decade, the exigencies of employment can require a man to crisscross the country, even move to other countries, in search of career opportunities. In European countries foreign workers admitted on contract provide services without which whole industries would collapse; in Switzerland they amount to one-fifth of the population, in tiny Luxembourg one-third.

Behind the massively publicized image of its desirability the family is beset by disintegrating trends. The status of the head and the duration of his rule are sharply circumscribed in practice, if not in theory. The precise location of his empire is subject to rapid and frequent changes. Even the social utility of the nucleus of parents and children is in doubt with an increasing number of studies and hypotheses showing the close relationship between mental illness, homicide and family relationships.[1] The groaning economic base of the nuclear unit can no longer be supported by the earning capacity of the head; he must be subsidized by tax concessions on his mortgage, allowances for his children, contributory income from the labor of his wife. The basic range of consumer goods to be found in most family homes has its own fragmenting and isolating effect, within the family as well as outside it. Two cars become common (so that conflicts over simultaneous use can be avoided); central heating means that all parts of the house are warm and usable (so that the family no longer congregates together in one room); deep freezers begin to penetrate the mass market (so that daily shopping and its inherent social contact become obsolete.) *One by one the familiar consumer durables of the twentieth century—led by the dwelling itself— have stopped off what were once enormous and necessary areas of social contact between members of the family and between families. The image of family life remains strong, reinforced by consumer advertising which it continues to dominate, but its reality is crumbling out of all recognition. The productive forces upon which it now leans are contributing overwhelmingly to its ultimate collapse. It is in any case already far removed from the organism described in the historic definition.*

---

[1] Statistics indicate that a significant increase in the murder rate occurs at Christmas—a notable time for family reunions.

The term community, "a body of people organized into a
political, municipal or social unity," betrays a similar dissonance with tradition when its contemporary form is analyzed.
Endowed historically with a strong geographical base, communities are now subject to the rapid population turnover
described above. The process of urban renewal which steadily
erases old neighborhoods and patterns of intermarriage by
demolition and dispersion, has facilitated the growth of large
suburbs within which nuclear families lacking any blood
relationship with each other pursue their isolated economic
fortunes. Between 1940 and 1960 the rural communities of
the United States, which were interrelated in this way, lost
over half their population to metropolitan areas with a minimum population of 50,000 persons. By 1970 sixty-five per cent
of the American population was urbanized, not in the sense
that it lived in the center of cities, but that it lived in *urban
areas*—the suburbs surrounding the decaying monsters which
are the reality of the big city image. The same pattern of increasing settlement size and decreasing indigenous population
is to be found in the United States, France, Germany, Britain
Japan, Scandinavia, everywhere that consumer society has
subsumed and vitiated the old "municipal or social unity" to
replace it with an *economy* of land and employment values
capable of overturning the purpose even of those parts of the
old provincial structure that remain. Small businesses in historic towns and cities subtly shift their servicing function to
cater to visitors rather than natives. Antique shops replace
bakeries, restaurants and hotels replace houses, chain bou-
tiques and stores replace the autonomous enterprises of former
times. The mediaeval town of Arles, in Provence, like many
others preserves its shell with its economy reoriented towards
the needs of visitors from as far away as the other side of

the world. A bitter notice at the entrance to the market reads "Tourist, you are in famous Provence, a country now colonized, polluted and despoiled: its language forgotten, its ancient traditions betrayed, its soul extinguished . . ."[2]

The centers of the larger cities are simultaneously gutted by long-term highway and renewal plans and abandoned by many of the major commercial and industrial employers whose presence alone makes the cost of maintaining urban services possible. Taking their jobs with them, the employers retreat to the suburbs where a new private life-style slowly starves the city of its cultural and entertainment facilities: one by one the cinemas, restaurants, night clubs and theaters disappear for lack of patrons. The remaining inhabitants, too poor to buy their way in to the suburbs (which are in any case defended against them by their middle-class occupants), exchange slum dwellings for subsidized apartment housing in ghettos where crime, unemployment and family breakdown haunt successive generations. Eventually the remaining private property owners in bankrupt downtown areas abandon buildings that can no longer command rents commensurate with the cost of maintaining services in wealthless but expensive neighborhoods.

Within the suburban enclaves themselves community expression finds its form in a variety of patterns of negative solidarity. The inhabitants of a suburb will band together to fight the invasion of their seamless web of private houses by bars, restaurants, laundromats; any kind of communal or public structure capable of generating "noise," "disturbance" or interference with steadily rising property values. The presence

---

[2] Lawrence Durrell, *International Herald Tribune,* July 19, 1972. The often remarked reluctance of small-town traders to support traffic by-pass routes proceeds from their understanding that the economic basis of their community lies *outside* not inside it. Many small American townships derive up to half their revenue from skillfully sited speed traps designed to catch the unwary drivers.

or threatened arrival of subsidized housing in the area demonstrates the community spirit of the suburbs in its clearest form. In the United States, news media have noted the proliferation of walled suburbs, many equipped with armed guards and elaborate electronic security systems. Bixby Hill World, in California, features automatic entry gates which can only be activated by inserting special tokens—numbers of which are mailed to guests when inmates throw parties. At Sugar Creek, near Houston, Texas, residents carry large identification signs on their cars, and fix similar badges to the collars of their dogs. Westlake Island, near Los Angeles, can only be reached by one guarded bridge.[3]

In Britain the juxtaposition of local-authority estates with areas of privately owned houses frequently produces conflicts only resolved by the construction of physical barriers between the two. The most celebrated case (though by no means the only one of its kind) involved walls seven feet high surmounted with rotating cast-iron spikes which were repeatedly built and demolished across such a divide between 1934 and 1959 at Cutteslowe in Oxford. In the United States, where suburban areas tend to be unfenced and landscaped, the enclave must be protected at its perimeter owing to the absence of internal barriers. The poor, blacks and other ethnic minorities are effectively barred from these white "spread cities" by illegal cartels of real estate agents and local vigilante groups more than prepared to firebomb any family that makes it through the outer defenses. Attempts to force the integration of schools by transporting children from the suburbs to the ghettos and vice versa are fought to a stalemate by legal delaying tactics and ambiguous political attitudes on the part of local representatives who know where their real voting support comes from.

The evasion of any area of public encounter, even the

[3] "Now It's Walled Suburbs," *Newsweek,* September 25, 1972.

everyday confrontations and showdowns of city life (pushing
for trains, competing for the waiters' or salesgirls' attention,
fighting for taxis), is a dominant characteristic of suburban
life.[4] It underlies the collapse of public transport in favor of
the private car, and in modern suburban developments such
as the British New Towns, it can be seen incorporated into the
very infrastructure of decentralization. At Milton Keynes, a
new city designated in 1967 and currently under construction,
the pattern of development will be based on eighty one-
kilometer-square neighborhoods, each with its own shops and
schools in addition to low-density housing. The area of the
city will be 22,000 acres and its population on completion
25,000. At traditional urban densities such an area could accommodate at least two million persons. The "center" of
Milton Keynes will be a massive 86-acre space planted with
7,500 trees and crossed by geometrical "boulevards" between
which will be located parking spaces for 25,000 cars.

Whatever notion of community underlies such planning
there can be little doubt today that the "political, municipal
or social unity" central to the historic definition of the word
has been totally reinterpreted. The dangerous dissonance between local politics—the issues that really engage the suburban citizen—and politics as presented at a national level,
which was so ably exploited by George Wallace in the early
stages of the 1972 American Presidential election (and which
is equally exploited by Enoch Powell in Britain and the major
right-wing parties in West Germany and Italy), shows itself
clearly at precisely those times when the community spirit is

---

[4] This evasion is nowhere more clearly evidenced than in the decline of
carol singing at Christmas time. Prior to the television age, this was a community enterprise with which august local figures were often linked. During
the last decade in Britain it declined into a form of blackmail levied against
TV watchers: "Pay up or we will sing." Finally (Christmas 1972) citizen
protests culminated in the inhabitants of some streets in Folkestone, Kent,
petitioning their local member of parliament to have carol singing banned
by law.

deliberately invoked. School bussing in the United States and immigration in Britain present clear indications of the depths of xenophobia and social fragmentation which underlie the silence of the majority. With their endless acres of arcadian development devoid of traditional urban interdependence yet bulging with the technology of private affluence, the high-turnover suburbs demonstrate a unique schizophrenia over political loyalties.

On issues such as foreign policy the personality of the candidate as revealed by television encounters establishes his popularity, and fed by media exposure and public-opinion polls his career can expand and contract in a blaze of publicity without his ever coming within striking distance of real political power. At this level the "political unity" of the suburb becomes a fantasy identification acted out over "issues" forgotten within months of a major election.[5] On local issues the position changes dramatically. In Britain, organizations of parents in London suburbs demonstrated and lobbied frenziedly during the spring of 1971 for security guards to be placed outside every primary school to prevent attacks upon children, which had not in fact increased in frequency prior to the furor. In the United States, 15,000 citizens of Berkeley, California, besieged the Mayor's office in 1970 with similar demand's for "block wardens" to defend their homes against "the dangerous revolutionary minority that has been doing its thing for six years." Violence breaks out over school integration, subsidized housing, and in Britain particularly over immigration. During the immigration scare of the summer of 1972, when expulsion of British passport holding Asians from Uganda threatened to create an influx of "up to a quarter of a million" immigrants at a time when unemployment stood at just under one million (the highest figure for a quarter of a century), the British government minister charged with or-

[5] See below, pages 124–5, for a selection of forgotten "issues."

ganizing the distribution of the incoming Asians disputed with local councillors on television. "We are all in this together," he began, only to be interrrupted by cries from representatives of areas already holding large immigrant minorities asking *him* how *he* was in it.[6]

The social unity of the suburbs is an infinitely graduated and eminently exploitable *disunity* based upon private criteria such as differences in the size of the mortgage, the hire-purchase debt, the age or charisma of the automobile and a hundred other distinctions visible only within the sign language of consumer commodities. The community unit is not the city, the suburb, the neighborhood, the block or the drive, it is the private connection with a worldwide credit and supply service, the freemasonry of the private owner. As such it has nothing to do with location in the sense of *belonging,* but everything to do with it in the sense of *receiving* that which is distributed throughout the land but more densely in some places than in others. The suburban community is a body of well-placed receivers on line to a massive delivery system. The stresses of city life impede the enjoyment of consumption; truly rural life with its remoteness, scarcities and absence of definitive peer groups checks ambition; only in the suburbs is the organization of what economists call "the intention to purchase" optimized, clarified and purified. Insofar as the exercise of consumption involves the adoption of similar states of mind and similar postures it is a communal experience, and suburban solidarity often takes the form of a group defense of postures and states of mind; but insofar as such solidarity only exists in relation to the supply of commodities, it is vulnerable to their scarcity. Even where the reality of affluence is less evident than its image, in the poorer pockets of the nations of the West such as Northern Ireland or Southern Italy, still

[6] Thames Television production, "The Immigration Question," on *This Week,* August 31, 1972,

the possibility of private wealth represents the sole real guarantee of social harmony under present conditions. In Northern Ireland, where the prospect of affluence for the Catholic minority was finally eclipsed by systematic discrimination in matters of housing and employment, the consequent disintegration of *all* the communities in the province proved more rapid and alarming than any observer had felt possible. The progressive subdivision of areas by means of bombings and demolitions, the erection of barricades and the construction of large numbers of miniature Berlin walls, all proceeded directly from the breakdown of the supply of commodities, including dreams. The physical juxtaposition of Catholic and Protestant families in Belfast, in some cases cemented by upwards of twenty years' peaceful coexistence, collapsed in an orgy of fire-bombing and evacuation within hours of the first major riots in 1969, and the process of community fragmentation did not end there. The creation of "No Go" areas (barricaded against security forces) in parts of Belfast and Londonderry in turn led to conflict between rival community groups, each claiming to represent the people of the area. Ultimately the formation of committees, movements, clubs and gangs split the effective administrative areas down from towns and parts of cities to streets, estates of houses, blocks of flats, even individual buildings and public spaces.

The efforts of the British administration to pacify the province without being able to first restore a belief in imminent prosperity have involved it—despite massive transfusions of investment for ailing industry—in merely contributing to this process of social dismemberment. The Protestant community, deprived of its government in March 1972, rapidly fell prey to the same proliferation of competing political organizations, each more extreme than its predecessor in the narrowness of its views of the whole crisis, and each consequently less likely to perceive the general lowering of horizon from city to town to street to individual family. In a tragic but utterly characteristic statement of the vacuum which lies beneath the dissolving social structure of Northern Ireland the mother of a fifteen-year-old girl tarred and feathered by the IRA for "espionage" told a television interviewer eager for evidence of sectarian bitterness that she took no interest in the outside world any longer, she knew nothing about it and thus could tell no lies. All she cared about was her own home.

The disappearance of the traditional concept of community is evidenced by its failure to reemerge under conditions of stress. The basic interdependence is gone because the whole technology of consumer supply, as well as the matrix of obligations and supports which constrained consumer ambitions, has changed from interlocking concentric circles to radiating lines. The linear structure of supply is monolithic and vulnerable; the seamless web of consumption, when starved of either its product or its product's image, does not so much fragment as dissolve. Community is gone, only wealth conceals atomization.

SOCIETY

Society in its contemporary Western form is thus held together by a pattern of aspirations somehow marketed alongside products and services whose social effects are demonstrably *fragmenting*. This paradox—which is nowhere implied in the Latin derivation *socius* (meaning "ally") nor in the 1553 definition "the system or mode of life adopted by a body of individuals for the purpose of harmonious coexistence"—can only be unraveled by some consideration of the overwhelming importance of economic factors in social organization today.

Since the Industrial Revolution and its attendant demographic changes the "system or mode of life" in the developed nations has been recognized as dominated by the principle of the division of labor; a fragmentation of the processes of production in the interest of increased efficiency which over two centuries and more has led to a complexity and differentiation in patterns of employment closely reflected in the modern system of labor mobility which underlies suburban living. The migrant suburban family, of the kind described above, survives in what C. B. Macpherson has called "a possessive market society"[7] entirely because it has willingly extended the fragmentary pattern of relationships which emerges from the conditions of employment out into all its social relationships—this is why Macpherson uses the term market *society* instead of market *economy*. Uncomplainingly it moves from suburb to suburb, even from country to country; friends are left behind, relatives unseen for many years, schools changed frequently. In all this it merely reflects the demands of the forces of production with minimal inertia and maximum compliance. The system of alliances (in the Latin sense of *socius*) that such a family builds up is filtered through the primary imperative of *employment* and this in turn derives from fluctuations in demand, investment and other factors influencing the market for the product or service with which the employed member of the family is involved.

Curiously, this slavish adaptation to market conditions has not brought about a balance between population distribution and the distribution of employment possibilities. On the contrary, despite increased labor mobility and increasing use of government money to finance the relocation of industry and commerce, there remains an irreducible conflict of interest between business prosperity and the perfect articulation of the worker's life-style to conform to it. There can be no one-to-one relationship; if there were, the competitive advantage—

[7] C. B. Macpherson, *The Political Theory of Possessive Individualism* (Clarendon Press, 1962). Macpherson argues that the key factor in what he calls a "possessive market society" is the existence of labor as a commodity apart from personality, a *possession* which the worker is free to hand over for a price.

which together with tax incentives, government loans and other penalties and incentives makes the whole operation worthwhile—would evaporate overnight.

Looked at in this light it is difficult to claim that social cohesion can result from such an arrangement, where even the final achievement of a unified pattern of mobility is unthinkable. Such cohesion as consumer societies at present evince must derive from other sources, or else amount to a form of resistance against the dominant social pattern of fragmentation. For if the social impact of the possessive market is conditioned by its demonstrable tendency to isolate and fragment, and yet a relatively harmonious pattern of social behavior still exists, then that "system or mode of life" must represent something other than the endlessly slicing effect of the productive machine.

Yet the trade union movement, the obvious example of a reaction against the divide-and-rule methods of mercantile capitalism in the nineteenth century, stands in an ambiguous position with regard to the forces of production. The doctrine of syndicalism, a theory for the total annexation of the forces of production by trade unions which once dominated the thinking of the French *Confédération Générale du Travail* (trade union council), is so far forgotten that its leaders, men whose predecessors published a scenario for revolution based on the presence of 100,000 striking workers in the streets of Paris,[8] themselves *prevented* such a revolution in May 1968 when already *ten million* French workers were on strike. An alliance exists not merely between trade unionists but between the trade unions and their traditional enemies the employers. The same alliance extends as far as the government—whether it be socialist or capitalist. In Britain the autumn of 1972 saw lengthy and serious negotiations between government, unions

[8] E. Pataud and E. Pouget, *Comment nous ferons la revolution* (Paris, 1902).

and employers over measures to contain inflation, increase wages and ensure economic growth. All three parties have the same overwhelming interest in common, the preservation of wealth and the dream of affluence.

The advent of *consumer* societies, in which the worker not only produced goods and services but provided part of the market for them, occurred parhaps half a century after the integration of syndicalist theory and has rendered much of it obsolete. The worker under these new conditions improved his status as mobile victim of the industrial cycle of boom and slump by becoming also a powerful consumer[9] whose purchasing capability is now vital to the continuation of the process of production itself. Workers who had once dwelt in close-packed city tenements and terraces began to find their class solidarity threatened by the accumulation of wealth of their own. Not wealth in the sense of the annexation of the labor of others, but *embourgeoisement,* the achievement of a status as individuals comparable to that of their middle-class counterparts. Living in their own houses, driving their own cars, their conditions of life conflicted with the role cast for them by such nineteenth-century thinkers as Marx, Engels and Sorel. Once they had been gripped by the vision of prosperity, the lure of revolutionary politics for the working classes in the West faded into a comparative insignificance from which it has not yet emerged.

The premature birth of a consumer economy in the United States during the decade preceding the Depression gave the American working class a taste of private wealth, with over 23,000,000 private cars (75 per cent of the world's total) owned by Americans in the year 1929. The 40 per cent drop

---

[9] George Katona, in *The Powerful Consumer* (McGraw-Hill, New York, 1960), argued that the restrained economic behavior of this new class of consumers prevented a slump in the United States after 1945, and that the largely untutored market intuitions of consumers as a whole exercises a powerful and beneficial damping effect on the American economy.

in gross national product which followed the Wall Street crash of that year threw over ten million out of work, and the employment situation only really recovered with the rearmament programs of the nineteen-forties. Nonetheless, revolutionary politics signally failed to draw the dispossessed away from the images of affluence glimpsed before the deluge. Sustained by the newly invented talkies (the most successful of which during the Depression years dealt with the random access to power and influence in high society of "ordinary people"), spectator sports, real-life gangster dramas, historical romances and radio programs, the American working class *endured* the Depression and more or less patiently awaited the return of prosperity. During the Second World War their liquid assets rose under the influence of high wages and compulsory savings schemes from 45 to 145 billion dollars. Boosted again by the production demands of the Korean War, these assets fueled the return of prosperity. In 1952 private house construction in the USA reached the record figure of 1,400,000 units; by the end of the decade the percentage of dwellings owned by their occupiers topped sixty-five: government-subsidized low-cost housing, initiated as a "socialist" measure in 1934 during the New Deal, still only accounted for one per cent of the total. By 1955 Detroit was selling to Americans every year as many cars as existed in Britain, France and West Germany combined. By 1970, figures indicated that this outburst of consumer prosperity had resulted in the population of the United States (just over six per cent of the population of the world) consuming forty per cent of the world's resources.

Such a process of material exploitation is Faustian in its irreversibility. There can be no halt, and, as we have seen, reversal merely lays bare the collapse of social cohesion of the traditional type brought about by prosperity itself. The social inequality which is guaranteed by industrial and commercial enterprise forever rules out any static configuration. Under the conditions described, only growth can act as a social pacifier. Increased production, increased wealth, increased distribution: all three mean that everyone is advancing, and the slower advancement of the majority is not greatly noticed. Besides, affluence involves the inclusion in the process of consumption of a wider and wider segment of society; even those who are moving most slowly become important in the context of the whole economy, no longer so much as producers, but as consumers of products. The recent growth of the *Volkswagenwerk* in West Germany clearly illustrates this process. In 1948 the company produced 80 cars a day with a work force of 8,000. In 1968, largely as a result of a powerful penetration of the United States market, production had expanded to the point where 5,000 cars a day could be produced by a work force of 43,000. Thus both production and employment increased, but the former at a faster rate than the latter. In 1968 five times as many workers were able to produce sixty times as many cars. At the same time the global expansion of Volkswagen sales had increased the total number of jobs created by car production to nearly a quarter of a million, with perhaps another million dependents supported by the activities of the company.[10] Under these conditions continued expansion is the only viable policy since any attempt to arrest it must decrease the efficiency of production itself by making more people effectively responsible for fewer cars.

Inevitably therefore even those forces in society dedicated to reducing its inequalities are obliged to advocate further growth; and those who oppose them to defend existing inequalities by pursuing policies which can only exacerbate them. Ironically economic growth does *not* reduce inequalities but merely masks them by further extending the already broad basis of consumption. The dynamism of the solution is precisely what prevents it from ever being finalized, but in the

---

[10] By 1972 it was calculated that one West German worker in twenty made his living from VW in one capacity or another.

event "perpetual motion" proves a better tranquilizer than any attempt to arrest the whole process. Clearly, therefore, any impediment to growth such as the economic retrenchment advocated by ecologists in recent years cannot have a socially stabilizing effect—quite the reverse. Like trying to stand still on a bicycle, the trick is harder than continuing to ride. What will emerge under conditions of arrested growth (wars of course are periods of *accelerated* growth, like freewheeling downhill) is not an access of patriotism, community spirit and family loyalty, but a social fragmentation so complete that the political forces representing the relatively prosperous are obliged to fight it at all costs—a defense which, in the context of a consumer society, involves the protection of the mass of consumers as well, perhaps fifty per cent of the population. Whatever protests governments may make about refusing to "yield to blackmail" in industrial relations when militant action leads to confrontations on this ground are simply bluff. Organized workers, who are key producers and key consumers, *are* enormously powerful in consumer societies, simply because they can upset the process of distribution of goods and services and thereby endanger the social cohesion which has become utterly dependent on these supplies. The tiny flutterings of unreliability which resolute industrial action causes to vibrate through the machinery of consumer supply, the days without newspapers, the blackouts and brownouts, the extended delivery times, the delayed correspondence; all these are harbingers of a collapse so total that they deserve to be greeted with the caught breath that accompanies a faltering engine on a lonely road at night. Consumer societies are like cars in that they have one complicated and vulnerable engine upon which all their functions ultimately depend.

The triumph and homogenization of consumer society has of course relied to some extent on the adoption of methods of economic management previously thought proper only to socialist regimes—an example of dialetic materialism which is unpopular with orthodox Marxists. But far more important than the mixed parentage of the Western economic system is the global success of its image of a consumer life-style. Facilitated by the enormous growth of communications media this global public-relations program followed rapidly on the heels of affluence.

Within a quarter of a century of the defeat of the Axis powers the development of communications technology and marketing has carried the message of "The American Way" to the farthest corners of the earth. Even where it scarcely exists the Good Life is avidly observed. Today Indian peasants gather round Japanese television sets to watch Yankee astronauts cavort on the moon. Vietnamese refugees, fleeing the advancing Northern army or indiscriminate aerial bombardment, struggle to balance stereo systems on the cross bars of bicycles. Weaponless African rebels carve imitations of sophisticated Western firearms, lavishing more care on the provision of visually important accessories such as butt plates and sling swivels than on ballistic performance.

The dreams of the underdeveloped countries are dominated by images of an affluent, suburban life culled from advertisements, tourists, movies and television series purchased and dubbed into more familiar languages. In Latin America, where a phenomenal rate of urbanization has left every major city with an outer ring of shanty towns, efforts to mobilize housing demand for revolutionary political purposes have achieved equivocal results. The *Pobladore* movement in Chile, once dominated by the left-wing *Movimiento de Izquierda Revolucionario* (MIR), saw its strong political organization of the squatter movement in Santiago dissipate with the achievement of security of tenure under the government of *Unidad Popular*. The *Pobladores* themselves already evince tendencies towards *embourgeoisement* altogether at odds with the ideals of their political leaders. At the MIR encampment of *Nueva Habana* Western delegates to the Chilean International Housing Conference of 1972 were shown a model of a house designed by the people of the camp. Complete with carport, porch, garden fence and private garden, the pitched-roofed, single-story, semi-detached house displayed a profound grasp of the imagery of suburban living on the part of people living five to a room in mud-floored huts. As in Cuba, the revolutionary government had abandoned self-build housing for this reason, adopting instead a method of labor conscription using ideologically sound *microbrigadas* of specially trained house-builders in an effort to head off dangerously bourgeois tendencies. In Cuba itself these *microbrigadas* construct small apartment blocks according to standard United States real-estate developers' plans which offer only two or three bedrooms per apartment, an arrangement totally at variance with the normal size of a Cuban family but consonant with the ideal presented in the context of international consumer advertising.

Throughout the world the image of future prosperity fostered by governments of widely differing ideologies differs hardly at all from the existence at present enjoyed by the consumers of the West. In a book[11] published in the USSR in 1959 the Soviet transport planner V. V. Zvonkov began a prediction of the pattern of Socialist automobile use at the turn of the century with the following:

'You want to go to Ensk?' asked the engineer Dolmatovski. 'Let me take you by car. I have the latest 2007 model.' We approached a silver machine with very small wheels parked outside in the street. The tapered back resembled the tail unit of an aircraft . . .

Another part of the book describes the interior of a Moscow apartment in the year 2000 with the same breathless enthusiasm. More recent Soviet publications chronicle the achieve-

[11] *Life in the Twenty-first Century,* edited by M. Vassiliev and S. Gouschev. Published in translation by Penguin Books, London, 1961.

ment of Zvonkov's dream. The March 1969 issue of Sputnik[12] for example describes the construction of an automobile factory:

The Volzhsky assembly plant at Togliatti on the Volga will be completed just 1000 days from the day when the first survey pegs were driven in to the steppe. According to chief designer Vladimir Solovyev, the first model produced will be the VAZ-2101, a slightly modified version of the Fiat 124. Solovyev said the plant will produce a car each 22 seconds—660,000 per annum . . . The prospective VAZ-2101 owner is likely to be a family man who wants to take his wife and children for a weekend in the country.

The development of commercial contacts between capitalist and socialist countries as well as the adoption of extensive economic planning in the West has served only to clarify the dominance of the consumer ideal in both camps.[13] The universal truths of our time are not ideological but acquisitive: people do not want to live according to *principles* but according to *desires*.

The social cohesion of Western consumer societies derives from the satisfaction of individual needs rather than from the conditions of life in a possessive market society, or indeed from the power of some atavistic folk memory of the past economy of scarcity. Affluence is not an *accidental* characteristic of the decentralized and transient patterns of settlement which dominate today, it is the one absolute essential for their continued harmonious existence. The romantic notions of the meaning of community which are repeatedly served up as evidence of the rebirth of an "alliance" among the economically and physically stratified citizens of the suburbs of the West

[12] *Sputnik* closely resembles *Reader's Digest* in format, just as *Soviet Weekly* resembles the old *Life* magazine. The resemblance is not accidental.
[13] Since 1965 American Express International has negotiated agreements over the use of its credit cards in Romania, Bulgaria, the USSR, Hungary, Poland and Yugoslavia. Pepsi-Cola now produces in the USSR.

are futile attempts to evade an irreversible historical process. Affluence has *permitted* social disintegration, or more accurately rendered it of small importance by substituting for it something else altogether, a new kind of social adhesive that works by dreams instead of realities. And if that means the social balance we possess is simply a product of affluence, and not the residue of something that affluence assails, then we must accept this and reconcile ourselves to its implications. There can be no turning back, for our antisocial society of non-community is a social form whose nature derives from the mechanisms and structures it employs to maintain the isolation of its citizens. The idea which is gaining ground in intellectual circles that under ecological and political pressure the process of growth and exploitation inherent in the nature of consumer society can somehow be reversed, betrays an appalling ignorance of the power of the simple idea of wealth.

Just as "Japanese capitalists can efficiently organize in six months an industrial political restoration that China's revolutionaries and Mao's best thoughts could not achieve in six years,"[14] so can a few years of VAZ-2101 production at the rate of one every twenty-two seconds make mincemeat out of whatever community structure might presently exist in the USSR. *Consumer society fragments, and universal consumer society fragments universally. The machines and the images do the trick unaided, not by inventing needs and persuading gullible citizens to work towards their fulfillment, but by providing the technology for those citizens to move out of the compound organism of "society" altogether. Which in the end, moralist and prophet of doom notwithstanding, is what they really want to do.*

[14] James P. Sterba, "Japan Tightens Grip on Asian Economy," *International Herald Tribune,* August 15, 1972.

CHAPTER TWO

THE PATHOLOGY
OF PRIVACY

Suddenly it seems as if those on the move will reap the benefits. There is no building for the future any more in the traditional sense, no putting away for later rainy days like those of the past—the only certainty is now. You can't identify yourself in terms of your environment any more because it keeps reconstituting itself—you'll find your castle built of sand. Self-identification can now only come from personal modes of action and not the things with which you surround yourself. Every kind of establishment is being questioned—you've got to move fast to keep a grasp; the accelerating rate of change is potentially the most democratizing force the world has seen. Use what you've got today —tomorrow you might find it obsolete, irrelevant, or worse, a strangling noose around your neck. The most precious thing in the world is *now,* because it's the only thing in your grasp. Your existential posturing will constantly shift— reality is only temporary. Never has living for tomorrow been more absurd; never has the future been more NOW.

From *Utility in architecture,* final-year thesis
by a London architectural student, 1970.

> We are facing the need for liberation not from a poor
> society, not from a disintegrating society, not even in most
> cases from a cabalistic society, but from a society which
> develops to a great extent the material and even the cultural
> needs of man; from a society which 'delivers the goods' to
> the larger part of the population. And that means we are
> facing the problem of liberation from a society where the
> desire for liberation has, apparently, no mass support.
>
> Herbert Marcuse, *Liberation from the affluent society*,
> Congress of the Dialectics of Liberation, London, 1967.

Apart from presenting opposed views of the possibilities inherent in an affluent society these two quotations display a
profound difference in the standpoint from which they were
written. The anonymous student wrote his thesis with no consciousness of a body of friendly readers. Not that he felt he
was expressing unpopular views; on the contrary, like an
advertising copywriter he uses the confident imperatives of
direct speech, "Quick! Get yours now!" The key is his use of
the pronoun of the second person singular as opposed to
Marcuse's use of the pronoun of the first person plural. The
student addresses his words to other grasping individuals like
himself alight with the guiltless consumer lust identified by
Marshall McLuhan twenty years ago.[1] The philosopher addresses himself to the obsolescent "we" of his audience, who
have "apparently no mass support" for their ill-starred rescue
operation. So deeply ingrained is the intellectual habit of
employing the mechanisms of the affluent society while deplor-
ing its behavioral and ethical base, that the irony of his position—evidently clear to Marcuse—escaped the notice of his
audience.

---

[1] "Consider the plight of the children of the rich. Life is dull for those
children who cannot share the collective passion of those who hope to be
rich. The speed, the struggle, the one-man fury are not for them." Marshall
McLuhan, *The Mechanical Bride,* 1951.

It should not, however, escape the attention of readers of this chapter, for the ironic quality of ostensibility underlies much of what is discussed here. This is because the idea that social changes of the kind described in the last chapter could only have come about with the active support of the populations of the countries concerned, is seldom accepted without a rider to the effect that those same populations were "confused," "misled," or "drugged" into a mindless compliance for the purpose. Rather than see the present behavior of consumer society as the inevitable result of a willful shaking off of the bonds of community, the "we" of Marcuse's audience prefers to view it as a "disease" with alarming symptoms, among them drug addiction, rising crime, militant industrial action, pornography, even inflation itself. The logical response to this "disease" theory is a "treatment" theory—since both derive from an entirely inappropriate medical analogy—and though the "treatment" prescribed by the supporters of Herbert Marcuse might appear to differ from that advocated by the technocrats of the political Right, the methodology employed to devise it must inevitably be the same because in this sense at least their viewpoint is identical.

Thus, for example, the process whereby the "sickness" of the cities of the West is "cured" by "cutting out the cancer" of the slums and replacing the "lost tissue" by an arrangement of hotels, offices and businessmen's pads, has exact analogies in socialist countries. The "crumbling capitalist heritage" of decrepit buildings in the central areas of the cities of Eastern Europe and Cuba is erased by ideologically different but otherwise indistinguishable structures. Other symptoms of the "disease" of community collapse are also dealt with similarly either side of the ideological frontier, but in all cases the significant thing is that the "treatment" always fails. If the purpose of urban renwal is to "transplant" communities living in unfit housing to more salubrious locations in the suburbs, then it can be truly said that the failure is spectacular. In the

United States studies have shown that one quarter of the families displaced by slum clearance are forced immediately onto relief and half the remainder find they can no longer survive on the principal breadwinner's income alone. One quarter of the businesses "transplanted" by the same process never open again.[2]

If on the other hand the purpose of renewal is to withdraw from the inhabitants of a given urban area the onerous obligations of community life, then it must be counted an equally spectacular success. The enthusiasm of the slum dweller for the prospect of suburban life knows no bounds save those erected by planners, political activists and urban community workers in their endless grapplings with the "pathology" of the voluntary desire for suburban anonymity. Attempts to retain "a sense of community" by rehousing slum dwellers in the same geographical areas by means of high-rise buildings which are physically isolating and often devoid of any community facilities, merely result in increasing difficulties for the teams of law-enforcement officers and community-midwife social workers who are drafted in to make good these deficiencies. The association of crime and vandalism with such ghettos is clearly attested by a 1971 report made to the New York Housing Authority which showed that delinquency increased in proportion to the size of such "transplanted" communities and in all cases was higher than in the slum areas previously occupied. Similar evidence of the breakdown of community obligations along with the traditional social restraints of urban life attends the new commercial areas which dominate the cities of the West. Writing of prostitution in New York, a journalist catalogues all the elements of this interaction:[3]

Consider the ingredients . . . new office towers, old celebrity hotels, the amoebic spread of massage parlours and "penetrating" triple X

---

[2] B. Zimmer, *Rebuilding Cities* (Quadrangle Press, Chicago, 1964).
[3] Gail Sheehy, "The Wide-open City" in the *Evening Standard,* August 4, 1971.

skin pics . . . add up the alliterative junk food parlours: Pizza Plaza, Zum Zum, Cobbs Corner and family . . . and the all-night drugstores which provide the aids to a hooker's trade. All of this crowned by Grand Central Station, crossroads of a million private lives intoxicated by the supermarket of American sex and convinced they are missing something . . . and what more does the flesh pedlar need? Cheap porn. The link between pornography and the infiltration of a new area by prostitutes is firmly established. One promises, the other delivers.

It's all coming together now . . . like one hellifying midtown planning project.

The failure of the whole process is in many ways reminiscent of a much more direct medical analogy from the history of surgery in the nineteenth century, a period of very great advance in human knowledge in general but laden with prejudice and self-deception like our own. During the 1860's, immediately prior to the adoption of antisepsis but after the introduction of anaesthesia, the survival rate of patients committed to surgery remained very low. Post-operative infections, in many cases attributable to viruses present in the hospitals themselves, killed nearly 50 per cent of patients subjected to amputations in general and two out of three of those made through the thigh—at that time a much more common operation than it is now. As a result a movement had gained ground in European medical circles which opposed the process of hospitalization altogether. Statistics of the period proved that the rate of survival for major surgery doubled in the case of small rural medical practices, even when these lacked modern equipment. Antisepsis itself, which reduced mortality by two-thirds or more, although demonstrated successfully in Glasgow in 1865, was not accepted in the major London hospitals until over a decade had passed. Resistance to it was led by the most famous surgeons in the land, by the British Medical Association, the *Lancet,* and even the advocates of hospital closure. The principle of antisepsis was adopted in Denmark and Germany before it was accepted in London. Thus even the demonstration of a fallacy by means of the most powerful statistic available, human mortality, failed to dislodge a persistent belief not in the superiority of traditional methods, but in the notion that high mortality through infection was an integral part of surgery.

The comparison between pre-antisepsis surgery and the "disease" theory of community collapse is obvious and compelling. The same fatuous adherence to methods demonstrably counterproductive is shown daily by planners, architects and sociologists in their efforts to combat a sickness which is in reality no sickness at all but the effect of unfulfilled desires. To the patient who complains of a pain in his arm the professional community planner offers a gas-powered limb. It is the hypothesis of this book that the *voluntary* factor in what radical and technocrat alike denounce as a disease far outweighs in importance any pathology involved. That, as a final invocation of the medical analogy,[4] the disease itself is drunkenness rather than alcoholism: an effect which is *desired* when we drink. *Illusions* of community parade through our lives masking a profound and guilty rejection of everything such a term should stand for if it retained any real meaning. Resistance to facts, even when clearly presented, is not confined to reactionary elements in either past or present societies, although it is part of the mythology of progress that this is so, for even the habit of referring to ourselves as "we" has become a confusing anachronism in a society of private affluence.

The great pop music festivals of the last decade for example, those quasi-mediaeval gatherings of the young, were in one sense attempts to recreate a sense of community along different lines from those employed by orthodox planners and sociologists. Their failure too owed as much to the insidiously private destiny of each participant as it did to a rip-off financial infra-

[4] For a more extensive exploration of the use of the medical analogy in planning and architecture see Robert Goodman, *After the Planners* (Simon and Schuster, New York, 1971).

structure or a hostile social environment. The pop revolution itself, always underpinned as much by nostalgia as by radicalism, erected a hypothetical "we" who would make us part of the natural world of childhood again in opposition to the "they" who preach nothing but the likelihood of economic, ecological or nuclear disaster. Perhaps because of its roots in drug culture Pop sees clearly the fate of the "use" of natural and cultural resources in the addictive disaster of "using them up." Perhaps the often remarked sadness of its music reflects the experience of failure in efforts to reverse this tide, for even when with enormous determination small groups of enthusiasts establish rural communes which eschew medicinal drugs, electricity, gasoline, canned and frozen food, they discover only ghosts—the ghosts of grim forebears obsessed with crops, labor, weather, and above all the compulsive theism of dependence upon the earth. To move back only one hundred years in methodology involves rediscovering not only primitive and exhausting techniques, but also the framework of ideas, beliefs and mores that made them part of a meaningful existence. The pace of life slows to a crawl, the significance of the individual diminishes into a pattern of hopes deferred for generations. The "we" of that past is a kind of living death acted out within earshot of rescue, within sight of jet planes and telephone wires. In itself it becomes the most unspeakable isolation; community appears farther away than ever, perhaps as far as it seems from a public housing ghetto.

I do not feel part of a group, a class or a country. All I know about myself is that I am a man born in the twentieth century. All I can talk about is myself.

This statement by a London photographer epitomizes the unregretted passing of the old patterns of group identity. Today there is no "we." To understand the songs and movements of the present a man or woman must, by an effort of will, dispose of the idea of community that seems to legitimize his or her existence. He or she must dispense with the easy "man," or "mankind," or "voter," or "taxpayer," or "consumer," or "middle class," or even "Western world." Not so completely as to make generalization impossible, but for a time so as to savor the absurdity of group identities that have become traps, pernicious illusions designed to conceal the awe-inspiring truth that there is now only the isolated resource-user and energy-expender: not the altruist but the self-regarder, not the lover but the orgasm-hunter. Every washing machine, every automobile, every deep freeze, every mortgage for every private house, every television set, every marriage, every affair, every policy (even insurance policies), all conspire to prove to us that our dearest wish is to flee the web of obligations for which the term "community" is merely a euphemism. Affluence and wisdom born of the self-image of television and record have destroyed the need and the desire for human interdependence: not in the manner of a sorcerer's tools run amok, but in the form of a sudden public demonstration of a secret wish. Today "we" find ourselves doing in the road what we could not previously believe that "we" did at all. Shocked, embarrassed and horrified "we" deny what I as an individual know that I have always wanted—to be irresponsible in the truest sense, to be without obligations, to be for myself alone.

To treat the conditions of life as though they were "problems," to set up committees, action groups and task forces to "solve" them, these are all in their way exultant abdications from the throne of real complicity in events. To see poverty as an anomaly, a "problem" and to try to sort it out by finding an "answer" to it is to deny its existence in the real world, to pretend it is some sort of accident and not the predictable result of things being arranged as they are. As an excellent French proverb puts it, when a thief is not actually stealing, he considers himself an honest man. So today does the individual—when he is not actually in pursuit of oblivion, nirvana, speed or orgasm—think himself to be part of a community which is somehow always there irrespective of his own actions. Recognition of the fact that this "community" (partly as a consequence of his own and his fellows' neglect) has become an illusion, an image, a roll of tape, a spool of film, a splendid but empty palace, is too painful. Hence the retention of the language and pageantry of community and obligation to describe an increasingly gimcrack façade of public events for which self-interest is the only comprehensible motivation. This massive self-deception, the best-kept secret of our century, is only betrayed by behavior, never by words—for "we" intentionally lack the words to describe it. Behavior in this sense has become increasingly divorced from the language that purports to explain it as part of the same self-protecting process. A triumph of security. Even under torture the prisoner cannot reveal his guilty secret, that he cares only for himself, that he does not know anything beyond his endless, inexhaustible self-obsession and the repeated actions that constitute his daily life.

Let us approach the same argument from a territorial standpoint. Surely the "we" we always use is a statement of identification based on the uniqueness of place, of language, of shared experience: a bundle of inalienable shibboleths inherited from home and street and school. To say "We are Germans" depends only on the recognized existence of a place called Germany. To say "we are Londoners" depends upon being able to differentiate a place called London. The process is identical with that which eventually differentiates the ego of the infant so that the grown individual knows what he is and what he is not. But supposing world trade, industrialization, urban renewal, media and mass travel have succeeded in making "Germany" much the same as "London": the buildings are the same, the cars are the same, the television programs are the same. "We" often deplore this overwhelming trend but curiously neither accept responsibility for it nor make the obvious extrapola-

tions. If everywhere is the same then the time must come when
we cannot say easily where "we" are—or, put in another way,
it will not matter. Beyond this it will not be clear *who* we are
either; for identity will come to depend on a narrow, interpersonal system of recognition. But here too identity is at a
discount, not so much through a general similarity between
careers, homes and possessions, as through a quickening dis-
continuity in the pattern of lives. As we have seen, American
citizens on average move house every five years, in Britain the
average mortgage lasts seven years, in the densely populated
quarters of cities the rate of turnover is faster still. Only a
modest acceleration of this trend would see every child moving
house four or five times before leaving school, with the result
that the only incorruptible evidence of identity would be the
agreement of friends or determined relatives that the child was
who he or she said they were. In the absence of a reliable "we"
even "I" become less certain—or put in another way again,
less important—for those very relationships which become so
crucial in respect of identity have at the same time become
onerous for other reasons. Community has always meant
responsibility, surveillance, concern for others—not so much
for their welfare, as many would pretend—but for their opinion, their judgment upon oneself. The "I" who comes to live
nowhere, who is known to no one and asks no one's advice,
who does not know who or where he is, is free in a sense that
was virtually impossible to imagine even a quarter of a century ago. Today his freedom is treated as a sort of pathology;
he is described as alienated, uprooted, lost, fallen, degenerate,
empty. Even those futurologists who less than a decade ago
excitedly predicted the coming of the citizen of the "age of
leisure" now fall silent with horror in his presence. Automation, the midwife of his birth, becomes suspect while economists, industrialists, union leaders and politicians desperately
sift through old economic miracles to keep him at work, in
the womb, a little longer.

Let us put aside the idea of a community pathology and

consider instead the suburban consumer who receives benefits from his goods in direct proportion to his expenditure on them, so much so that it makes sense for him to work overtime, to get his wife to work (if she does not want to anyway), even moonlight, doing two jobs one after the other in order to buy more. For him the socially divisive effect of a consumer life-style cannot be accidental but must, on the contrary, be passionately desired. Once equipped with the basic range of consumer goods such an individual never retreats from them; quite the opposite, his appetite increases like that of a drug addict so that the sort of car that satisfied him in 1970 must be somehow "better" by 1973, likewise the television set, the stereo system, even the home itself. No intrinsically unrewarding process of manipulation could bring about such compulsive self-amortization. *There is something about the economy of means by which such cheap implements as the refrigerator, the TV and the car can undo the social patterns of centuries that makes them seem like tools designed especially for the job. These things were* designed *to reduce human contact, to reduce the amount of time spent worrying about the goodwill or hostility of others.* With his armory of inanimate energy slaves no individual need concern himself with the interlocking obligations of community, family or social life (the telephone for example is at least as useful for not having to *see* people as it is for making contact with them). Nor need he fear the isolation of outlawry, for he and all his fellows are already outlaws insofar as they are indifferent to the supposed moral force of law. Literally millions of motorists commit offenses against the law every day, as do ticket bilkers, income-tax fiddlers and welfare chiselers.[5] Consumer equipment has

[5] Henri Lefebvre (*Everyday Life in the Modern World,* London, 1971) takes an orthodox pessimistic view of this phenomenon. He writes, "Each individual trembles lest he ignore the law but thinks only of turning it to his own advantage by laying the blame on someone else." [We live in] "a society where everyone feels guilty and is guilty—guilty of possessing a narrow margin of freedom and adaptability and of making use of it by stealth . . ." But see below, page 196.

been designed to facilitate and tranquilize this lawless isolation. The escape from community obligation is the real payoff of such a life-style. It is the overwhelming benefit that outweighs a lifetime of forward debt commitment. It is a choice, not a trick. The community has said "no" to community: it prefers fantasy instead.[6]

This much having been said, it should occasion no surprise that the guilty "we" (which is all of us) refuses to exult openly in its new state of "I." The ancient community of language reinforces our guilt, for it contains only complicated word structures to express the *absence* of community rather than its opposite. Our guilty secret is sustained, too, by a willing suspension of disbelief at least as great as that whereby the Church withstood the death of God. Not only do we wish to exterminate community, but we wish to do it secretly. Privatization has become the Final Solution to all our social "diseases" and our profoundly ambiguous attitude to that solution is reflected in the evasive thinking that surrounds it.

"We" are a society of private citizens, given over to private goals and private pleasures. We are self-absorbed and we prefer it. Do not judge us by our community rhetoric, look at us instead. To us community means obligation, surveillance, aggravation. To us privatization means a media-fed life of autonomous-drive slavery wherein every wish is gratified and every fear calmed by means of sublimation. Our supplies of consumer goods ensure that we can sublimate any desire somewhere within the massive supermarket of available commodities, or if we cannot satisfy it we can at least take away our appetite with something else. That is what consumer

---

[6] The London *Times* for April 10, 1972 contained a report to the effect that the television comedian Mr. Leslie Crowther had criticized the "disgraceful hypocrites of Aldershot" who ignored a charity show put on to raise money for relatives of the seven victims of an IRA bomb attack on the barracks in the town. Only 250 people attended the performance in a 1,500-seat cinema although the cinema next door showing a James Bond film was filled to capacity.

goods are for. Their ostensible functions are in reality subordinate to their overwhelming function as social isolators.

Whole forests of advertising copy attest to the "cheapness," "convenience," "quality" and labor economy of consumer goods. Their functional design is praised, the status they confer is gloated over; every possible facet of their use is dwelt on except their primarily antisocial purpose. Just as no distiller in the world dares to advertise his whisky with the simple claim that it makes you drunk, so no manufacturer of consumer goods dares to stress the ineffable release from interpersonal obligation that his product represents. One might expect sociologists to present a gloomy assessment of the growth of antisocial tendencies, but advertisers, who gain proportionally, should surely grow increasingly exultant with the passage of time. Alas, they remain modest, as does the manufacturer and even the designer (who of all people should understand the purpose he is so assiduously working out). Remorselessly coy, implacably euphemistic, they refuse to face the triumphant vindication of their life's work.

THE CAR—"LIKE BRINGING A WOMAN TO ORGASM"

Take the automobile, a paradigm among consumer artefacts because it explains so much about what we really want for ourselves. It has long since ceased to represent a convenient means of transportation; hedged about with legal and economic restrictions, the conditions governing its use grow steadily more intolerable, the machine itself has become increasingly unreliable and, if only through the enormous improvement in its performance, more dangerous. Still its popularity does not wane. Like a small spacecraft, a satellite of the home that is air-conditioned, fantasy-styled, filled with stereo music and quasi-useless control systems, the car thrives on components designed only to last the length of the manufacturer's warranty period. The maximum effective life it can claim is that laid down by the corrosive chemicals applied to road surfaces in cold weather, which consume its fabric in proportion to the intensity of its use. Even lavish precautions against rust cannot protect the body of the car for more than a decade because the combination of metals used in its construction, as well as the differing consistency of single metals, guarantees that electrolytic action will carry out the process of decomposition in any case.

This self-destructive property is important chiefly because it has demonstrably had no effect on the popularity of the automobile. Far from being a practical tool, the car has become a self-renewing system for absorbing income, but in the process the nature of its appeal has become unclear. The conventional wisdom is to assume that model recalls, escalating warranty costs, notorious unreliability and dwindling life are unfortunate accidents which temporarily plague the evolution of the perfect dream car. Accusations are leveled at workers who "take no pride in their work," at cheeseparing designers who seek to maximize profits by minimizing material, at reliance upon post-delivery remedial work, and so on. In fact even massive recalls like the seven million Detroit cars returned to the manufacturers for repairs in the first five months of 1972 (more than the number retailed during the same period) have little or no effect upon the market. Ford Pintos—of which a quarter of a million were recalled following flash fires in air filters during 1971—topped minicar sales for the first six months of 1972. Torinos and Montegos—of which half a million were recalled in the spring of 1972 because their rear axles and wheels actually fell off—continued to sell well in the latter half of the year.[7] In Britain warranty work—repairs to cars during the manufacturers' twelve month guarantee period—accounts for 25 per cent of all repairs carried out by garages,

---

[7] "Detroit recalls a recall," *Time* magazine, May 8, 1972.

costing an estimated £55 million to car owners.[8] Obviously the durability and mechanical performance of the car has little to do with its popularity, an assumption borne out by the annual progress of the British magazine *Autocar*'s readership surveys which have noted a steadily declining interest in purchase price, resale value, servicing cost and fuel consumption[9] since they began in 1969.

Clearly we buy cars for other reasons than their practicality. The likelihood of death or injury through motoring similarly disposes of any notion that a feeling of security is derived from them. In Britain, analysis of accident figures led to the forceful comparison between driving to work twice a day and balancing "on the parapet of a twelve-story building in wind and rain and dark, perhaps with your children trustingly holding your hand."[10] In the United States, the automobile is the leading killer of persons under twenty-five, and has in fact killed nearly two million individuals since the turn of the century—far more than all the wars undertaken since independence.

Used generally as arguments in favor of expensive safety modifications, just as pollution arguments are used to justify the largely gestural adoption of low-lead petrol and the expensive development of prototype electric cars, these figures are far more convincing simply as indices of the enormous *value* which the contemporary citizen places upon his car. Today we buy cars because they are *private* technological worlds (increasing sales of small two-door cars have been noted by American manufacturers), about which we can worry and fantasize and hover and in the end dismiss—as mediaeval kings did their court favorites—in favor of new ones, exactly the same but different. It is only in such psychotherapeutic terms that short-life, unreliable and dangerous automobiles

[8] Alisdair Aird, *The Automotive Nightmare* (Hutchinson, London, 1972).
[9] "You and your car," *Autocar,* July 20, 1972.
[10] "Kerbside Grand," London *Sunday Times Colour Magazine*, October 11, 1970.

make sense at all. Like the sounds of masques and operas at the courts of *anciens régimes* the roar of the exhaust—or perhaps the beat of the in-car eight-track stereo—muffles the cries of anger, despair and anxiety without the palace. For the car is a palace, in the same sense as the private bathroom. Both of them separate, encapsulate and remove certain aspects of behavior from the public eye. Thus the driver enclosed in steel and glass, only partially visible, presents a uniform exterior, clad in armor, frozen to a posture, arrogant, invincible, modest or simply rich. His movements become a therapy for sublimation, a series of physical exercises in coordination become outer manifestations of an inner life, a cerebral existence of which the pedestrian observer can know little. The confrontations with fear, danger and death that driving brings are uncommunicable private experiences, like the songs and masturbations of the bathroom. Bathroom and car are liminal spaces, somewhere-between states, neither present nor absent yet infinitely *possible*. And it is in this technological approximation of the existential state of being that the charisma of the automobile is to be found. More than the freezer, the television set, the vacuum cleaner, the central heating and air-conditioning system, the automobile is the shibboleth of privatization; the symbol and the actuality of withdrawal from the community; the gift of wheels.

Fears of the breakdown of affluence have served only to increase the dominance of the automobile. Never has the wonderland of the driving seat been more necessary than now, when to commute between flat and office, office and airport, airport and hotel, is to articulate the elements of a life that would become diffuse and gray otherwise. Without the car as insulator, the car as personality, the car as accumulator, the car as reflex-tester, the car as therapy, the elements of consumption-oriented life might run together in a disastrous disorientation or worse still remain defiantly apart, refusing to be welded into a coherent whole. The role of separating mechanisms such as the car and the home is crucial and continuous. All the parts of the consciousness of private man must be kept alive and in some sort of relation to one another, but they must not touch. It is a trick as difficult as walking a tightrope. Having a car can help you do it.

Only if his fuel runs out need the driver face the reality of the rest of the world on its own terms—then, and when some mechanical breakdown brings his dream machine down through the ages of man from space orbit to walking on his feet along amazingly extended freeways devoid of habitation or human scale. While it lasts, the automobile confers the priceless analgesic of *distraction,* a thing like silence that we are prepared to pay almost anything for. Apart from its physical therapy the car confers a new perception, a new viewpoint from which the landscape is both distorted and discriminated into negative or affirmative symbols, a priceless simplification of life. Listen to Clive Trickey[11] of the automaniac magazine *Car and Car Conversions* as he tests "the most beautiful, fantastic road car you ever did see. Long, low-slung, sleek, elegant . . . the 1963 250GT Lusso."

Gently I engaged first gear and moved away. My greatest compliment is that within five minutes I felt completely at home with this exotic beauty. It fitted like a glove and responded to every whim. If I dozed it dozed in unison, waffling along quite happily at 15 mph. But a quick flick through the gears and a stab on the accelerator and the waffle was gone, the tach whirling madly to a rising crescendo of sound as the occupants were thrust back into their seats. 100 mph was seen in a few yards—and it was still accelerating like a mad thing . . .

Off he goes, playing his mechanical bride like an old Stradivarius, riding a set of sensations (Jackie Stewart is only the most famous driver to have discovered the metaphor relat-

---

[11] "A Feast of Ferraris," *Car and Car Conversions,* November 1971.

ing cornering to "bringing a woman to orgasm") and studying
a set of signals remarkable chiefly for their spare lucidity:
HALT, YIELD, GIVE WAY, DO NOT ENTER THE BOX
UNTIL YOUR EXIT IS CLEAR, NO STOPPING and so on.
The car is something to see from, so the noise, the fumes, the
cities torn down to make way, the accumulated indestructible
junk, all can be ignored because they are a part and yet apart
from its central purpose, which is to *enable* things to be
ignored, put to one side, deferred until tomorrow. Driving is
movement, and movement is the evasion of consequences,
details and peripherals.

The automobile consumes energy and confers privacy and
distraction just as a fire consumes energy and confers warmth;
its relationship to the older forms of public transport is exactly
that of central heating to the open fire. Alone and distributed
into a mobile limbo the driver shares the freedom of the individual who can go anywhere in the house because the whole
house is warm. The automobile as a paradigm is important
because it can be used to illustrate several of the characteristics
of that *ostensibility* which is the hallmark of contemporary
social praxis. The car masquerades as a functional appliance
when in fact it is a psychotechnical, almost-human robot more
amenable and yet more dangerous than the most amazing
lover. Perhaps the driver is modest, perhaps cornering is *better*
than "bringing a woman to orgasm." But here we leave conventional analysis behind, not because politicians and commentators fail to acknowledge the mysterious grip the automobile exerts over human imagination, but because their conception of the relative roles of control and volition in modern
life is so inexact as to compel them to explain automania too
as a kind of disease instead of a festival of sensory overload.
Tediously it is denounced (like divorce and drug addiction)
as though it bore only a *pathological* relationship to "real life."
When of course, as any one in the commuter queue will tell
you, it is one of the few things that makes "real life" worth

living. Experiments between 1960 and 1962 to probe the motivations of drivers,[12] using hypnosis and hallucinogenic drugs, revealed that "escape to solitude alone in a car, with the heater on and the radio playing," together with a strongly competitive racing instinct, lay at the very foundation of most drivers' attitudes to driving. Simple observation of social intercourse between drivers shows that it equally underlies their mode of introducing or evaluating their own and others' machines.

The fact that increasing numbers of people purchase increasingly expensive and short-lived vehicles all over the world reflects the overwhelmingly rewarding quality of motoring: to denounce it as a disease is to fail to understand the real importance of the difficulties under which it takes place. The hazards and restrictions governing motoring today serve really as a camouflage to mask guilty indulgence in a massive pleasure, an irresponsibility without parallel. The car is a social diving suit, an isolating personal environment. All cars are getaway cars.

This being so, the restriction of automobile registration through limitations on use in cities, increasingly expensive anti-pollution devices, more elaborate safety features and steadily increasing cost is likely to be a losing game. Britain already possesses twice as many vehicles per mile of road as does the United States, and almost three time as many as Japan. Nonetheless the rate of increase of registrations is such that a doubling is expected to take place before 1990 in all three countries. The notion that such a manifest demand can be stayed by increasing costs and appeals to reason is utterly without foundation, and yet, because the reasons for automania are everywhere misconstrued, such "treatment" will be applied—together with punitive measures—to the same level of absurdity as currently obtains with official efforts to stamp out marijuana smoking. Because the antisocial effect of both

[12] Stephen Black, *Man and Motorcars* (Secker and Warburg, London, 1964).

practices is thought to be self-evident, abandonment is conceived simply as a matter of recommendation with mild pressure. Once it is grasped that the antisocial effect is *desired,* the real nature of the "problem" can be seen—and the futility of the pursuit of a "rational" process of repression easily proved through the marijuana analogy.

POT SMOKING: THE CONSUMER GETS HIS WAY

For the sake of brevity let us limit our consideration of this practice to the phenomenon of pot smoking in college. This activity has undergone a steady increase in popularity over the last decade—an increase moreover which has been directly proportional to the intensity of official efforts at discouragement. Taking the official view of the dangers of the practice, massive indulgence by an assumedly intelligent *élite* can only be explained by one of three basic arguments. First that these "intelligent" people are really stupid, so their "intelligence" (as attested by their presence at a university) must have been assessed on the basis of "stupid" criteria—an argument which throws the entire value of university education into doubt. Second, that they are (despite their agreed intelligence) in the grip of evil "pushers" whose real aim is the destruction of civilized life as we know it—thus their desire for the drug is simply evidence of the extent to which these ruthless men have enslaved them. This argument generally leads to demands for "protection" for students to save them from evil influences. Third, that as a result of their stress-free, milksop infancy (the product of hard-won victory in two World Wars) today's students are possessed of a kind of *faiblesse* which makes them strangers to character or ambition: inevitably with such people the dangers of marijuana act as positive inducements to indulgence, at least until the chance of a more permanent degeneracy at the hands of harder drugs comes along.

Now, each of these "explanations" for pot smoking in college posits the existence of an evil far greater than pot smoking itself as proof. In the first, intelligent people are really stupid—an alarming enough conclusion. In the second, the universities are riddled with the agents of organized crime. In the third, the morale of an entire generation has collapsed to the extent that it wishes nothing more for itself than euphoric death. If either or all of these are true then one can only admire the *sang froid* of the observers who know these facts but refrain from more drastic efforts to overcome them. If pot smoking means stupidity, thought control or a death wish then the future of Western civilization does indeed hang in the balance. In this connection it is instructive that no amount of "scientific" evidence as to the innocuity of the drug can shake the confidence of its opponents in their analysis. President Nixon himself denounced the findings of the National Commission on Marijuana and Drug Abuse before it had even begun its study, assuming that its work was destined to lead to conclusions even more pernicious than the findings of the contemporary Commission on Obscenity and Pornography, which he did not denounce until its report had been published.

Two factors emerge clearly from the above analysis. First, that in official circles any explanation for pot smoking which involves conspiracy, criminal exploitation, mental illness or danger to the fabric of civilization is inherently more credible than any counter explanation seeking to minimize the significance of the phenomenon itself. And second, proceeding from it, that such exaggerated fears inevitably lead proponents of the banned activity to revise upward their assessment of its social significance. Thus university pot smokers have come to believe that their modest habit *is* in some way connected with world revolution, consciousness expansion and the crack of doom for consumer society. *It is necessary to move out of the context of affluence altogether before one can see that pot smoking is an entirely characteristic product of consumer society, a part of the Western system of social fragmentation for private satisfaction and pleasure; a necessary corrective to*

the stresses and strains of a collapsing public life. The revolu-
tionary students of Latin America for example see marijuana
as a typical tool of Yankee imperialism which is cynically
employed by that government to damp down demand for real
social change.

In the Netherlands, where the voice of the socialist party,
Radio Vara, broadcasts, a regular market report on marijuana
and hashish prices in the same general context as stock market
figures and advertising for consumer goods of all kinds, overseas fanatics complain of an apathetic conformity in the
behavior of the underground. In France, where attempts to
suppress drug taking have reached such a pitch that Article
L.630 of the law of December 31, 1970 provides prison terms
of up to five years for the ill-defined offense of "presenting
narcotics in a favorable light," there are no such complaints
about apathy but many fear that the crack of doom is percep-
tibly nearer than in Holland.

The arbitrary illegality of one form of private nirvana does
not separate it from other forms. Driving and pot smoking are
analogous fantasies, analogous pursuits of private pleasure.
The discouragement of one and the acceptance of the other
merely displays the confusion and damage caused by failure
to accept the reality and irreversibility of community collapse,
and the consequently *vital* social role of products and practices
currently denounced as trivial.

Consumer goods today determine social realities; they are
the only reliable guide to income, life-style and aspirations.
The marketing formula A, B1, B2, C, D, E is as definitive as
the Hindu caste system for the purposes of any consumer
society. Do you own a car? A central heating system, a clothes
drier, a dish washer, a dry shaver, an electric blanket, an electric stove, an electric iron, an electric kettle, an electric floor
polisher, an electric food and drink mixer, a gas stove, a gas
or electric refrigerator, a hair drier, a household radio, a stereo
system, a record player, electric space heaters, gas space heaters,

oil or paraffin space heaters, a tape recorder, a television set, an electric toaster, a vacuum cleaner, a washing machine, an electric toothbrush? Do you have a bank account, credit cards, investments? All these things fit in and around your home, which has become a kind of consumer envelope for the purpose. All these products—whose saturation of the mass market is steadily plotted on graphs and statistics in a thousand advertising agencies—represent nails in the coffin of the old "we" that we still think we are. The increase in their use parallels exactly the closure of theaters, cinemas, night clubs, railroads and bus services. There is no difference in their social effect from that of perfect contraception, pornography, an ideology of personal liberation, a marijuana cigarette or even a heroin needle,[13] for these are merely the *products* of a second generation of decommunitized citizens, equally enthusiastically consumed.

Thus the consequence of marijuana prohibition merely illustrates the consequences which can be expected to result from attempts to restrict the use of private cars. The delinquent practice will not itself be stopped, far from it, but a pattern of paranoia laced with the savagery of unnecessary punishment will supervene in yet another area of public life. Tendentious "research," massive propaganda and savage penalties no more extinguish pot smoking than they extinguish road accidents. Cars and pot deliver the goods; there can be no other explanation for their widespread and increasing use. To ignore this simple deduction is to open the door to endless philosophizing about social pathology, public madness, alienation and reduced social capacity. Yet it is precisely this door which is not only unlocked but forced off its hinges by an enormous

---

[13] The total failure of the United States government to reduce illegal imports of heroin is significant in this regard. Federal Bureau of Narcotics and Dangerous Drugs (BNDD) estimates for 1971 showed that 6 tons of heroin worth $3 billion were imported in that year. In 1973 the BNDD estimated 8 tons, worth over $5 billion, would be imported, despite the activities of 1,500 special agents in all parts of the world, an annual budget of $70,000,-000, and increasingly severe penalties.

volume of psychiatric testimony, fruitless legislation, research and special pleading.

The blame for this situation can be squarely attached to the propagation of the myth of community and its embodiment in the routine denunciations of the "pathology" of corruption and materialism in modern life. As was the case with Nazi Germany, and later with the acquiescence of the American people in the atrocities of the Vietnam War, the notion that some kind of *disease* lies at the bottom of the non-appearance of public outrage raises more questions than it answers. Far more logical —if less comforting—is the alternative view that the rewards to be gained from affluence, from the supremely magical products of private consumption, are commensurate with the suffering and injustice that runs on unchecked because of them.

In a sense choices made by the peoples of the West—for the private car and against public transport, for suburban life and against urban or rural community, for owner occupation and against tenancy, for the nuclear and against the extended family, for television and against the cinema and the theater, for social mobility and against class solidarity, for private affluence and against community life, for machine politicians and against charismatic leaders, for orgasm and against conception, for eroticism and against reproduction, for pollution and against regulation—all these are choices in favor of privacy, in favor of individual freedom, in favor of anonymity, but against the very idea of community. The triumph of consumer society is a triumph of all private goals over all public goals. *The citizens of consumer societies are apolitical in so far as they are independent, political only when their lines of supply are threatened. Thus when energetic governments interfere with the supply of marijuana for their young people, those young people become politicized in precisely the same way as the homeless have become politicized all over the world. The demand is indiscriminate and the politicization is merely instrumental: the result is that the consumer gets his way.*

CHAPTER THREE

THE PSYCHOLOGY OF PUBLIC WITHDRAWAL

If living in the suburbs, driving your own car, owning your own house and listening to perfectly recorded music on your own stereo headphones are examples of the pleasures available to the private citizen, they certainly do not constitute an exhaustive list. Nonetheless some indication of the strength of demand for such privileges is given by advertisements in the classified columns of newspapers and magazines. "I made 3,000 monthly in mail order . . Evenings only!" "Make 1,000 per cent profit bronzing shoes." "Eliminate debts. New credit fast and easy. Ironclad guarantee!" Or, for those more conscious of their inadequacies, "Win $100,000," or "Find buried treasure!"

Educated to believe himself free to take his chances at any one of the neon-lit saloons of free enterprise, the Western citizen finds himself instead to be at the mercy of bureaucratic administration remarkable (in a global context) only for its refusal to adopt a coherent ideological stance: the kind of bureaucracy in fact that he was confidently told only existed outside the "Free World." During his own lifetime the same citizen discovers, more by direct experience than explanation, that the tentacles of this administrative system are continually extending their grip so as to threaten the manipulation of his entire life-style according to a number of generalized principles derived not from central theoretical works cheaply published and widely disseminated, but instead from "research" carried out in secret and applied apparently indiscriminately—not so much in accordance with need as with opportunity and predictable lack of resistance In the West the application of "behavioral control" cannot be identified with a general theory of popular good because the inequalities of life are too obvious to make any such goal credible; instead, *ostensible* goals are chosen and propagated. "Growth rate," "balance of payments," "productivity," "inflation," all are abstract terms that can be discussed without at the same time referring to the fluctuations of an *individual's* fortunes under their influence. The discussion of unemployment in percentage terms instead of absolute figures is a case in point. And yet the correspondence between extensions of bureaucratic power and new consumer opportunities is not really obscure. The doubling of vehicle registrations which took place in Britain between 1960 and 1970 brought with it a vast proliferation of regulations governing driving, from an overall seventy-mile-an-hour speed limit to metered parking in almost all towns and cities. Similarly the mushroom growth of credit finance that powered the consumer boom of the same period imported a massive increase in public surveillance by agencies created with the sole purpose of accumulating data on individual creditworthiness. "Freedom" itself, the magical element in Western social praxis which supposedly differentiated it from others, came to require an extension of the powers and numbers of those employed to defend it to such an extent that the withdrawal of the citizen from one public arena after another became a necessary and central theme of mid-twentieth-century life.

All these clearly contingent developments lack only official acknowledgment of a general causality—but that acknowledgment remains the one element which cannot be supplied. In its place we find the concept of the "credibility gap," the formulation designed to express the disbelief of the populace in the utterances of their administrators, and at the same time their refusal to denounce them simply as liars since such a denunciation would imply action of the most strenuous and unsettling kind. The duplicity has become as it were institutionalized and largely accepted. It is almost as though the people prefers its administrators to be guilty so as to legitimize its own profound indifference to general principles of egalitarian justice. The scepticism of the Western citizen as regards his politicians, administrators, managers and functionaries legitimizes his withdrawal from general concerns into private ones. For public life to become corrupt, self-serving and tyrannical it is necessary that the vast mass of the population should acquiesce in the process; if the vast mass of the population does so acquiesce, it offers evidence that public life is not a central concern, that administration can be viewed as it were at a remove from those things which are really important. Thus the easy accusations of corruption and incompetence have in fact become evidence of *complicity*, evidence of the irrelevance of rule to the majority of the population.

This process can be clearly seen by comparing instances of administrative interference in two assumedly very different social and political contexts. Both examples are taken from news reports, one following President Nixon's visit to the Chinese People's Republic, the other a roughly contemporaneous incident involving urban redevelopment in a British provincial city. In one case the resultant interference with the lives of the individuals concerned is legitimized by the invocation of a greater general good, an ends-justifies-means argument. In the other the suffering is not so much justified as *explained* by administrative incompetence. In the West the explanation is as satisfactory as the justification in the East. In the East the explanation is unnecessary because the justification is complete.

Barbara Walters talked with her interpreter, a bureaucrat who had been sent with his wife to the country to work with peasants. Their three children had been left behind and the interpreter was now uncomplainingly separated even from his wife.[1]

The sad saga started three years ago when Swindon Corporation told families living in Hinton Street that their homes were threatened by a bypass plan. Seventy-six of them sold up to the Council and left. But a few days ago the Council voted to accept a new route . . . A Council spokesman said that families who left could buy their old homes back. But they would have to pay the current market price—nearly twice as much as they were paid two years ago.[2]

Superficially it is arguable which arrangement produces the greater atrocity: the "mind control" which enables the Chinese to accept the apparently random fragmentation of his family, or the uniquely Western combination of socialist planning with capitalist consequences. In the Chinese case the justification involves the assumption of a willingness on the part of all citizens to "do anything that is beneficial to the people,"[3] a general theory within which minor inconveniences assume their "correct" proportions. In the British example the explanation is conversely very specific; the chairman of the relevant subcommittee is reported to have said, "It is a shock-

[1] NBC reporter Barbara Walters visiting Peking with President Nixon's press entourage in February 1972. *Time,* March 6, 1972.
[2] "Road Plan Killed Street by Mistake," *News of the World,* London, July 6, 1972.
[3] A Chinese schoolgirl of fourteen on her ambitions. *Time (ibid.).*

ing thing to have happened and eventually someone must take responsibility for it." No general principle such as a theory of planned urban renewal is invoked, instead the event is described as "shocking" and the principal consequence envisaged is one of blame, "eventually someone must take responsibility for it." This is the language of guilt and failure mixed with the hope of a *personal* evasion of responsibility, the classic Western pattern of scapegoatism. No suggestion of the impossibility of making omelettes without breaking eggs.

The paradox is now clear. In the West the general principle is submerged beneath layers of guilty complicity based on the unspoken assumption that interference with the livelihood of the individual is unthinkable and if it happens the only reason must be a "mistake," a "shocking thing." The center of the matter is not susceptible to generalization; each incident is an *absolute* disaster for which someone must be responsible. Consider another example, this time from the United States.[4]

Roger McAfee, a white farmer, put up 405 acres of his family's 1,100-acre co-operative farm near Fresno, California as collateral for the remaining 100,000 dollars [required for Angela Davis's bail] . . . "I'm just a working man who agrees with the philosophy of Angela Davis," McAfee said. Then he left the Palo Alto jail to return home "because I have to milk my cows." His homecoming was not pleasant. No sooner had word of his deed on Angela's behalf got out than his four school-age sons were expelled from school, ostensibly on the grounds that he no longer lived in the school district, but in fact, admitted the principal, "under tremendous pressure" from the community.

Here the explanation offered by the school principal embodies the same exculpatory elements and provides the same transparently unsatisfactory rationale—a deception somehow thought necessary by the outraged citizens of Fresno and

[4] *Time,* March 13, 1972.

obligingly, though half-heartedly, provided by the headmaster of their school. "The community" requires an explanation, not a justification, because an explanation is good enough. Indignation over such events is confined to a minority who must in any case drive themselves to apoplexy in efforts to rouse the same emotion in others when the whole structure of public reaction demonstrates the profoundly guilty indifference of a mob the morning after a lynching. In the West the omelettes being made are private omelettes and eggs broken are public eggs. By such deceptions is the immaculate omelette conceived.

This principle is not confined to isolated incidents, which though frequent in their occurrence, might not be thought of sufficient moment to arouse public rage in any case. The "problem" of rising crime—itself arguably the result of the increasing number of acts thought worthy of proscription—has produced a similar structure of specious arguments, scapegoats and ill-considered measures—not justified but "explained." In Britain, after eight years' deliberation, a Criminal Law Revision Committee produced a draft Bill in the spring of 1972 intended to greatly increase the powers of the prosecution as a means of curbing the number of acquittals recorded in trials by jury during the previous decade. The Committee suggested that the mandatory warning of the right of silence during police interrogation in practice had the effect of limiting the chances of a successful prosecution in the case of "hardened criminals" with previous convictions who, acquainted with police procedure and secure in the knowledge that their previous convictions could not be brought to the notice of the court until they had been judged guilty or otherwise, could thereby evade justice. Statistics were produced in support of this hypothesis which purported to show that almost half the accused in criminal trials who had pleaded "not guilty" during that period, had in fact been acquitted. Following in the wake of a number of successful indictments of police corruption, chiefly involving bribery and the fabrication of evidence, this draft Bill provoked some criticism, partly on account of the short period allowed for comment from the legal profession (a mere two months compared to the eight years occupied by the preparation of the Bill itself), and partly on account of the remarkably specious nature of the statistical evidence offered. According to this, proceedings on indictment against 12,700 people during 1970 had resulted in 6,324 acquittals—clear evidence, claimed its supporters, that justice was being thwarted. According to the Bill's critics the 6,324 acquittals included cases where people were wrongly charged, where charges were withdrawn, where acquittal on some charges was accompanied by conviction on others, and where judges had directed acquittals. Excluding these anomalies the figure of absolute acquittals fell to less than half the claimed figure. Related to the total number of persons proceeded against irrespective of plea during the same year the percentage of acquittals dropped from an emotive fifty to an unremarkable six.

Against the centuries-old tale of the evolution of criminal law such hasty improvisation as is exemplified by the proposed abandonment of the police caution, the right of silence, the concealment of previous convictions and the inadmissibility of hearsay evidence, seems scarcely to justify eight years' gestation. On the contrary it smacks of instrumentality—the desire to achieve a higher rate of convictions, a greater *efficiency* in police work—and this of course was its real purpose. The fact that such specious reasonings should be presented in the majestic context of the law reflects nothing so much as *an indifference to the complex matters of principle involved* and a corresponding enthusiasm for the simple punishment of "responsible" persons. Thus the thief becomes responsible for the inequality of wealth, the demonstrator for the manifest consequences of social injustice, the traffic offender for road congestion, and the humble pot smoker for a variety of social ills extending from anarchy to violent crime. "Rising crime" is institutionalized by "tougher measures," and the mechanism of law enforcement papers over the cracks in the principle of justice which has ceased to matter.

Such measures, or measures of the same generic type which have been observed in recent years in the area of unwarranted searches for drugs and dubious charges of conspiracy in relation to political protest, have persistently failed to "stamp out" crimes of the kind they were invoked to deal with. The failure is structural in the method and the method itself fails because it is an ostensible rather than an actual response to the problem. In short it is a camouflage. It does not solve the problem because it merely provides an "explanation" for the officials who are blamed for it. A proliferation of laws creates a proliferation of criminals, and responsibility for dealing with them creates scapegoats among administrators who are paid to solve such problems. Thus the administrator devises "tougher measures" which in turn create more criminals whose existence in turn demands further "tougher measures." Major social changes such as a redistribution of wealth are ruled out from the very beginning for reasons which must be already clear. Instead the majority interest is served by the energetic erection and development of substitute programs, which in their apparent failure to work do in fact very successfully maintain the *status quo*—albeit at a steadily increasing cost. The complicity between the private citizen and the government which he regularly denounces as "incompetent" is revealed on precisely this ground. The Western world will beat a pathway not to the door of the inventor who devises a better mousetrap, but to that of the theorist who promises a new or better method of defending the *status quo* by devising new and improved methods of control which postpone the need for social reorganization. The remorseless failure of each successive panacea serves only to encourage the inventiveness of potential successors. Such is the pattern of ambition and achievement in the service of the state of private affluence.

Under the conditions outlined by this hypothesis the real function of such expensive and unsuccessful activities as the attempted prohibition of marijuana by the governments of the West reveals itself in a new guise. Its ostensibility grasped, its real purpose becomes clearer. Condoned deception at this level is *an integral part* of administration in the West, it is a characteristic of public life. The higher up the political ladder one searches, the more flagrant examples are to be found, from the sober assurances of stability that precede currency devaluations to the routine absurdities with which successive administrations chronicled the progress of the Vietnam war. The same level is maintained by the outlandish claims of even the most modest advertisement, by the statements often made about the earnings of popular entertainers, even by so simple a device as the prerecorded interview. Not that there is much moral significance in the phenomenon: its very universality places it on a par with bribery in other parts of the world—an aspect of reality that people either come to terms with or not, according to opportunity and temperament. It does, however, have an effect on the politically supine citizen who is none the less at the mercy of politicians.

The conventional wisdom in such matters is to assume that, confronted with transparent but determined duplicity, the individual at first becomes cynical and later either sinks into indifference or begins to speculate with greater or lesser enthusiasm on the *real* reasons for the things he hears about. In fact his reaction is somewhat more complicated because it involves the admission of a third character, an intermediary between the citizen and the untrustworthy administrator. A person whom, in deference to the German novelist Peter Handke, we will call the goalie. Handke's novel *The Goalie's Anxiety at the Penalty Kick*,[5] is a study of the relationship between language and reality and of the distortions and de-

---

[5] Translated from the German by Michael Roloff (Farrar, Straus & Giroux, 1972).

ceptions of language as it simultaneously describes and obliterates experience. Although the author did not have the attitude of the individual to the unreliable behavior of his rulers in mind when he wrote it, the image which this extract conveys admirably illustrates the complexities of a process everywhere regarded as straightforward.

If you looked at the goal-keeper [in a soccer game, instead of looking at the players] it seemed as if you had to look cross-eyed. It was like seeing somebody walk toward a door and instead of looking at the man you looked at the doorknob.

This is precisely the predicament of the individual who views the utterances of officials and politicians with suspicion —since he knows they are not to be believed—but who cannot afford to ignore them either. The fact that people do not believe what they read or hear is actually far less important than the fact that they do not wish to act on their disbelief. Having elected a group of thinly disguised lobbyists for this or that sectarian interest the people cannot totally ignore their play because power is real (as well as corrupting) and those in power may well change the rules of the game if they are not closely watched. How then is the consumer to monitor the game if the corrupt players continually rend the air with cries of "goal!" and "foul!" to camouflage their own sordid accommodations? The answer is the goalie, who is the communicator, the commentator, the link man, the advocate. The goalie is a member of the team like the players, but he has found a way to flash signals to the audience. The difference between a television "performer" and a television "personality" is to be found right here. The apparently undistinguished, middlebrow, easygoing, frequently boring television personality is a spy. He is an employee of the television company, of the interests the company represents, of *the system* in its widest sense. But the secret of his success, the reason the public loves *him* and not the hundreds of other hopefuls who are (or were) his competitors, is because really he works for them, looks after them, he is *their* goalie too. If they should let their attention wander to the players, via involvement with community affairs or political activism, then the invaluable armor of their scepticism is lost and the pain of deception begins all over again. The goalie is part of the reason for the enormous value of the television set to the consumer. More valuable by far, because of its continuous monitoring capability, than any newspaper or magazine can be. With television it is not the program that is important, certainly not the substance of the news. It is the *sound,* the background blur of voices that like the ticking of a clock or the cyclic 'ping" of sonar is only significant when it changes, or when it stops.[6]

Reliance on the goalie is an important element in the security system that has made possible the substitution of an anonymous servicing network for the cloying attachments of community. For the consumer, life-servicing goods can reduce the anxieties of isolation to a point where they too can be quantified as a part of the "rent" that must be paid in order to retain the concomitant freedoms. With his own home, his own car and his own freezer the consumer can pare down involuntary social contact to the level of the regular payment of bills. Equipped with the electronic watchdog that his television receiver has become, he is able to narrow down the area of his vulnerability to something like the size of a goal mouth— through which the cannon balls of external reality cannot burst without some warning.

The droning voice, night after night, week after week, resembles the noise of a car engine. But like the engine of a

---

[6] The German magazine *Stern* sponsored a test in 1972 in which 184 people volunteered to give up watching television for a year as an experiment. The first subject to break down lasted three weeks, the last five months. The loss of television made all respondents irritable. Ninety-three per cent admitted hitting their children during the experiment as opposed to 78 per cent before.

car, any change in its note has significance. If the note is smooth and even, the subject and the substance can be ignored. Thus the television personality can be admitted to a cage of snarling radicals without waking the supine suburbanite. David Frost confronts militant miners, rioting Yippies, unrepentant junkies. He stands alone between Jew and Arab, Catholic and Protestant. Is he in any danger? No. How do you know? Because the tone of his voice does not falter, it is always the same. You do not even need to listen to the words to know that everything is all right, you have nothing to fear from miners, Yippies, junkies, Arabs or Irishmen—at least not yet. Between catastrophe and the consumer stands the goalkeeper, a man who is paid an enormous salary which he deserves— anyone who remembers Richard Dimbleby's handling of the Cuban missile crisis on BBC television will recall how one night everything seemed to hang on *the tone of his voice.* Ralph Nader, Johnny Carson, David Frost, Dick Cavett, Jack Anderson, Walter Cronkite, John Chancellor, Harry Reasoner —watch the goalie,[7] he will tell you when a shot is coming your way.

It is in this way, watching while not really watching, listening while not really listening, that the individual citizen uses television. In this sense all media, not just television, privatize rather than publicize. The shrieking headlines, the wail of sirens and the roar of bombs on the news, the stutter of machine-gun fire, all are less important than that subtle monitor, the tone of voice that accompanies them. Far from being "a window on the world" the television set is a periscope by means of which the submerged suburban viewer sees and understands without either seeing or understanding. Interposed between the maelstrom and the private citizen is the goalkeeper, as important a component in the world of simul-

---

[7] Significantly, both Nader and Cronkite were voted higher in public-opinion polls dealing with public credibility than either of the U.S. Presidential candidates for 1972.

taneous electronic communication as the transmitting station itself. Anyone who doubts this hypothesis should take the time to compare the voices of newscasters and commentators of the period of the Second World War and before with those of today. Between 1939 and 1945 particularly, a high-pitched, urgent voice commanded attention, heaped abuse on enemies, extravagantly lauded allies. Today a relaxed, objective tone discusses such matters at a remove. The change is obvious and startling, and as in other matters it is not accidental. The real vulnerability of the war years has given way to the real invulnerability of the nuclear *détente* and the well-armed police force, and the change is reflected in the sound of the media motor.[8]

In many ways the dual role of the television newscaster and commentator is as much reflected in political mistrust of the medium as it is in public enthusiasm for it. The endless debate about the meaning and significance of television does proceed in part from a genuine bafflement over the imponderable social influence of electronic communication, but to a far greater extent it results from the curious alliance which has grown up between old-style politics and old-style print journalism against the new medium which appears to threaten them both.

The decline of print advertising and the absolute decline in newspaper readership which have taken place as a result of the impact of television, both provide newspaper proprietors and journalists with every reason to oppose its growing power and influence. At the same time the uncertainty with which politicians view television campaigning, their tendency to blame it indiscriminately for their own failures as well as the successes of their opponents, encourages them to act wherever possible to limit its independent role, even though they show no lack of enthusiasm for it as a simple vehicle to advertise their own

[8] The collapse of Walter Winchell's career as social commentator in the early 1960's owed much to the increasing dissonance of his urgent voice in an era of relaxedly confident competitors.

policies. In consequence, newspapers tend to expatiate at length on the destructive social effects of television, and indeed to employ television critics who specialize in a "diagnostic" approach to the dangers of the medium,[9] while politicians with increasing skill evade the actual arena of television debate in favor of prerecorded talks and party political broadcasts. The combined effect of these measures is to inhibit the medium which a decade ago was confidently expected to bring about an era of clean politics and make possible the true, instantaneous democracy of the electronic plebiscite. Whether there is any connection between the secret function of the television personality and the birth of this anti-television alliance remains to be seen. The probable destiny of all centrally controlled media, which are inherently vulnerable to this type of attack, will be discussed in a later chapter.

If we assume, for the purposes of the development of the present argument, that the private citizen does in fact conspire with his corrupt government and self-serving politicians in order to justify his own social inactivity, then we should also expect to see this process reflected in his attitude not only to politicians, policies and public works projects backed by the state, but to human relations in general. A clue to the essentially negative watch kept on public life by the private citizen has already been found in the ambiguity of the role of the television commentator, but much clearer examples emerge

---

[9] During 1972 British newspapers for example, hard pressed by declining advertising revenues and increasing labor and material costs, devoted an increasing proportion of their coverage of television matters to "probes" into the effects of "violence and pornography" on television. The London *Evening Standard* in particular gave increasing space to its television critic Milton Shulman, who with pieces entitled "The Half-truth Machine" and "Keep off the Box, Mr. Heath" led himself into such an extreme position of denunciation that he welcomed the decision of the House of Commons not to permit an experimental screening of debates with the announcement that any institution which permitted itself to become involved with television was "defiled" by the process. In a televised discussion he repeatedly attributed the present low status of politicians to the machinations of this evil medium.

from a study of public reactions to major industrial and engineering projects whose predecessors were able to enlist the enthusiasm not merely of local communities but of whole nations.

During the Middle Ages in Europe the construction of the immense Gothic cathedrals which still dominate many cities was carried out by specialized craftsmen over a long period of time and at great expense. Popular enthusiasm for these enormous projects, comparable in cost and dubious utility to the space programs of 800 years later, was remarkable and consistent. The Abbé Suger wrote of nobles and common folk alike acting as draught animals to haul stone from the quarry at Bézières for the completion of the west façade and the northwest tower of the cathedral at Chartres. Whole villages took part in the labor of transporting lime, stone and food for the workers on carts pulled not by animals but by the people themselves. The Chartres phenomenon rapidly spread to other areas of France and similar activities took place in Germany and England.

This form of spontaneous public support survived well into modern times. The railway boom of the nineteenth century bore witness to a similar outpouring of popular enthusiasm, largely in the form of investment. The first decade of the twentieth century in Germany saw the aeronautical experiments of Count Zeppelin, whose whole fortune had been expended on the construction and testing of giant airships, saved by a phenomenal burst of popular support in the shape of a "National Airship Fund" which came into existence in the aftermath of a particularly dispiriting crash in 1908. As late as 1930 the round-the-world flight of the most famous airship of all, the *Graf Zeppelin*, was partly financed by a special stamp issue.

No such evidence of popular zeal has accompanied the development of the supersonic airliner, which might reasonably be assumed to be the successor to the mediaeval cathedral and the zeppelin. In the United States, despite a great deal of lobbying on the basis of employment prospects, Congress failed to allocate funds to the projected SST in 1971. In Britain the progress of the Anglo-French Concorde has been marked by signs of increasing popular disapproval. Noise problems, escalating development costs (from initial estimates of £150 million to current figures of £1,000 million), predictions of commercial disaster, failure to agree on air corridors, all attest to an unprecedented want of enthusiasm for a national prestige project. Gloomily newspapers enumerate the alternative uses to which the money could have been put: for less than half, a hovertrain network could have been constructed, for just over half, half the Channel tunnel could have been bored; for the same sum four subsonic airbuses could have been designed and built. The SST, like the prospect of interplanetary travel, has failed utterly to capture the popular imagination in the manner of the Gothic cathedral or the zeppelin. Perhaps, as Roland Barthes[10] has observed, the automobile is the true successor to the cathedral—in which case the fall of the community project dissolves neatly into the myriad private satisfactions we have already discussed.

CHILDREN: THE PRODUCT YOU LOVE TO HATE

Within the pattern of individual relationships the effects of social withdrawal and private pleasure are as evident as the lack of enthusiasm for community or national projects cited above. Family relations are, as many commentators have observed, under almost unbearable stress during the normal

[10] Roland Barthes, in *Mythologies* (Paris, 1967), wrote: "I think that cars today are almost the exact equivalent of the great Gothic cathedrals: I mean the supreme creation of an era, conceived with passion by unknown artists, and consumed in image if not in usage by a whole population which appropriates them as a purely magical object."

course of daily life in any consumer society, and in consequence much evidence for the decline of the institution itself has been gathered and published. Crime, violence and mental illness can be reliably linked with—if not explained by—the intergenerational warfare of the parental home and analogous difficulties resulting from the demands of a sexual morality utterly at variance with the massive propaganda of eroticism to which all consumer societies are subject. The magical status accorded to consumer goods themselves, as a result of their successful truncation of the necessity for dependent social contact, has in many ways transferred itself to the pattern of relationships between individuals who lay the same heavy expectations upon one another as they have learned to lay upon their domestic and transportation machinery. The consequences of this process can be clearly seen in the evolution of attitudes toward children since the Industrial Revolution.

Middle-class sentimentality notwithstanding, the relationship between children and their parents has not always been one of love—nor has the dominant parental motive been one of joyous sacrifice. Two centuries ago the introduction of popular education in England via charity schools, workhouse schools and Sunday schools was in part at least impelled by a desire that children should be taught to *work* as well as to read and write, with the former activity commencing as early as the age of five. So frequent were disputes between parents and workhouse masters over the children's earnings that in several cases it was found necessary to turn day schools into evening schools so that the children could remain at work during the day.[11] As the iniquities of child labor progressed into the nineteenth century so did the economic value of the child increase. Factory work was carried out equally by men, women and children; so much so that the chief ground of

---

[11] B. Kirkman Gray, *A History of English Philanthropy* (Cass, London, 1967).

opposition to the Ten Hour Act of 1847 (which limited the hours worked by women and children) was that it would equally limit the hours worked by men because the factories could not continue to operate on their labor alone.

As late as the year 1914 the most callous exploitation of child labor by parent and employer alike was the rule rather than the exception wherever it was possible to get away with it—as it was on the land. There a child might receive the equivalent of 5p an acre for stone picking; a boy of thirteen 15p a week for working 60 hours; a mature man 65p for the same. A consequence of the humanitarian legislation which effectively extinguished this pattern of interdependence was that for the first time it rendered ambiguous the formerly exploitive relationship between parents and children. Families whose immediate ancestors had unquestioningly relied both on the labor of their children and on their support during an unsubsidized old age, began to suffer unusual strains when both parenthood and retirement became the concern of social legislation and the public purse. Family allowances, free education, tax relief and pensions freed children from a direct involvement in their parents' struggle to remain alive. Instead they spent longer at school, and in some countries came to be fed, medically cared for and ultimately found empoyment by commercial and government agencies.

With increasing force after World War Two, social mobility exaggerated this effect; as did a rising incidence of divorce and separation among parents contribute to a new attitude towards parenthood itself. Writing in 1947 of the effect of wartime employment upon young mothers, Eustace Chesser[12] noted that in many English working-class neighborhoods the evacuation of children from areas vulnerable to air raids had led to mothers becoming accustomed to living independent lives with their own earnings "and thus resenting duties to

---

[12] Eustace Chesser, *Unwanted Child* (Rich and Cowan, London, 1947).

home, husband and children—which without the intervention of war would have come about naturally in their turn and received natural acceptance." The consequence was "a surprising increase in sheer feckless neglect of children's well-being and appearance." Twenty-five years later a London nutritionist confirmed the tendency which in 1947 was barely visible. According to G. W. Lynch of Queen Elizabeth College, London,[13] only 28 per cent of children in the affluent southwest of England are adequately fed, as opposed to 50 per cent in the poorer northern parts of the country. The more affluent the family the worse the diet of the children, not because of misapplied income, but through a decreasing interest in the whole subject. Emphasis on convenience foods and the abandonment of the old-style high-protein breakfast merely mark the beginning of a tendency towards the abandonment of cooking as a family activity. Already in the United States many children get their meals not from mother but from refrigerated vending machines at school after heating in microwave ovens. The development of the synthetic-food industry, using soyabean protein, peanuts or haricot beans to make anything from steak to chicken, promises a further extension of the industrialization and depersonalization of food supply—a further reduction in the parental bond.

Characteristically, middle-class families contrived to mask the disintegration of their own dependent interest in their offspring by means of an "explanation" rather than a justification. The evolution of parental indifference or even positive hostility was for a long time obscured by the adoption of a "permissive" mode of child-rearing owing much to Dr. Benja-

---

[13] In a broadcast on Welsh television on May 4, 1972. Confirmatory evidence was supplied in the U.S.A. by the 1973 Senate Select Committee on Nutrition and Human Needs, before which body Dr. Dean Mayer, nutrition professor at Harvard, testified that "Parents were partly to blame" for yielding to TV advertisements for sugar-coated breakfast cereals which are mostly "empty calories."

min Spock, whose theory that the child should be allowed to develop his or her own patterns of behavior and learning as a result of free or advised choice instead of command and discipline, consorted well with the domestic priorities of a family concerned first and foremost with material escalation. The child's "free choice" became instead an effective neglect under the comforting name of freedom.

This neglect, however, is not simply the reverse side of the coin of the child's value as a worker. The child is not spurned because he no longer contributes to the family income and is no longer necessary as an insurance against old age. Instead he is *ignored*. There are other, more pressing matters which require the attention of the principal breadwinner. A recent study in the United States involving research into the childhood background of thirteen radical students indicated that in all cases libertarian motives were not the principal reasons for the freedom to which they became accustomed during their childhood. Far more important was "a desire on the part of their fathers during the affluent fifties to be free themselves to earn more money or advance their careers."[14]

If attention to his earning capacity provided the father with an excuse for his indifference to the upbringing of his children, the escape of the wife and mother from redoubled obligations has proved to be a far more complicated and bloody business, involving the birth of an instrumental theory of female emancipation. "Few can have observed recent developments without being convinced that the emancipation of women has reached a stage where it is a danger to society," observed Dean Inge in 1930—at which date women could still be committed to insane asylums for the "crime" of having illegitimate children. Twenty years later David Riesman noted further contradictions in the "emancipated" mother's role. Fed with libertarian propaganda she learns that "there are no problem children,

---

[14] Robert Rath and Douglas J. McDowell, *Thirteen Counter-Culture Families* (Pennsylvania State University, 1971).

only problem parents . . . She looks into her own psyche whenever she is moved to deny the child anything, including an uninterrupted flow of affection. At the same time she is told to "relax" and "enjoy her children," even this becomes an additional injunction to be anxiously followed."[15] Twenty years later still the results of such fulsome propaganda have become statistically significant. Jessie Bernard quotes U.S. Department of Health, Education and Welfare figures to show that married women are twice as likely as married men to commit suicide, and one Boston study shows that over sixty per cent of the suicide attempts recorded were made by housewives with children. "Children decrease rather than increase domestic happiness," she concludes; "school-aged children, six to fourteen, have an especially distressing effect."[16]

Studies in current middle-class attitudes to marriage—which are carried out with an instructive (and obsessive) regularity by magazines and newspapers—repeatedly stress the role of parenthood as the ultimate "explanation" for the continuance of an institution which would otherwise become an unrewarding mutual tyranny of legal and financial obligations. From the foregoing it is evident that *even with children* that is exactly what marriage has become. In Britain 500 children die every year from injuries inflicted by their parents; suspect wounds lead medical authorities to suppose that perhaps 11,000 every year suffer some sort of attack. Perhaps the most significant part of the evidence offered at a 1972 conference on the subject held in Britain was that the guilty parents display no generic abnormality. "So far no particular ethnic or religious background has proved significant. There is no common psychiatric category into which these parents can be placed."[17] In other words they are normal.

[15] David Riesman, *The Lonely Crowd* (Yale, 1950).
[16] Jessie Bernard, *The Future of Marriage* (New York, 1972).
[17] Paper delivered by Carolyn Okell of the battered child research department of the National Society for the Prevention of Cruelty to Children to the Royal Society of Health annual congress 1972, Eastbourne, England.

The whole structure of women's liberation is necessary to extradite the trapped mother and wife from this oppressive situation; the father and husband escapes by concentrating on his work and displaying the rewards of his earning capacity— a washing machine, a freezer, a small car for his wife. The tyranny exercised by the child over the household is made possible by the irreducible element of guilt which afflicts both parents: the father is guilty because he allows the child's infancy to slip by while he concentrates on other things; the mother is guilty because popular mythology says she is supposed to give the child everything and yet however hard she tries she cannot ever give him enough to produce a commensurate gratification. To clearly face the issue by recognizing the child as a fraudulent piece of merchandise, sold to her by a combination of commercial hucksterism and oppressive tradition, requires a remarkable brand of courage and confidence. The "wonderful free offer" of a child is a hangover from times that she never knew but was often told about, when "human relations" were different from relations with products or services.

The child, of course, becomes aware of the real meaning of the combination of guilt and obligation that passes for family love. As he or she grows older the very process of growth exacerbates parental rage over the "chances" missed because of the obligations and duties of parenthood. How much better for the child to be an additional breadwinner, a worker, a slave for the good of the family, than to be a "teenager," a "student" an idealistic "young person." How necessary for the child to escape from parents whose belated concern for him or her at maturity is really self-concern—lest the ungrateful offspring staying away from home at night, taking drugs, committing crimes, getting pregnant, might bring shame, disgrace, even expense upon them by getting into "real" trouble.

"The Lonely Crowd"[18] of 1950 has become the "Nation of

[18] Riesman, *op. cit.*

Strangers" of 1972, and the evidence of family disintegration adduced by Vance Packard in the latter study[19] closely corroborates the sententious comparisons of Dr. Bronfenbrenner in his celebrated eulogy of Russian child-bearing.[20] According to Packard half the 18- to 22-year-olds in the majority of American towns are living away from home with no intention of returning. This "disaster" he attributes to the pervasive influence of mobility, which he proposes should be counteracted by limiting the powers of large corporations to draft their employees from one facility to another, guaranteeing minimum incomes to cut down the migration of workers in search of more pay, encouraging home ownership, and so on. All of these measures require a major reorganization of the economic structure of any developed country in the West (with the exception of the encouragement of home ownership which in any case is no bulwark against mobility, as figures cited by Packard himself clearly show). The pathology of Packard's "accelerating rootlessness" is based on his own indictment of "nomadic values" such as hedonism and a tendency to live for the moment, and his enlistment of dubious sociological theories attesting to the "lowered social capacity" of the nomads themselves, who are apparently "indifferent to all close associations." Which is to say that they refuse to condemn their own life-style with the same enthusiasm as Packard himself. The value of Packard's study consists in his correct identification of the mobility of young people with the possession-oriented mobility of their parents. The unspoken assumption of many other social critics that the desire of the young to leave home and keep moving amounts to a reflection of parental values is nonsense. It is a trick that they learned from their parents—just like the trick of ignoring each other.

Bronfenbrenner takes a more sentimental and less moralistic view of the same group of social phenomena. In a splendidly

[19] Vance Packard, *A Nation of Strangers* (McKay, New York, 1972).
[20] Urie Bronfenbrenner, *Two Worlds of Childhood: USA and USSR* (Russell Sage Foundation, New York, 1970).

unconscious explanation of *why* half the 18- to 22-year-olds are living away from home he reminisces about the good old days:

On the good side, some of these relatives were interesting people, or so you thought at the time. Uncle Charlie had been to China. Aunt Sue made the best penuche fudge on the block. Cousin Bill could read people's minds (he claimed). And they all gave you Christmas presents.

But there was the other side. You had to give them all Christmas presents. Besides, everybody minded your business. They wanted to know where you had been, where you were going and why. And if they did not like what they heard, they said so (particularly if you had told the truth). And it wasn't just your relatives. Everybody in the neighbourhood minded your business. If you walked on the railroad trestle, the phone would ring at your house, and your parents would know what you had done before you got back home. People on the street would tell you to button your jacket, and ask why you were not in church last Sunday. Sometimes you liked it and sometimes you didn't—but at least people *cared*.

But what does *care* mean? Does it mean this:

Crystal Lynn Awbrey, age 16, N.M.Y.L. File no. 164. Left home 10/5/70. Born 8/26/54. Ht. 5′3″. Wt. 125 lbs. Nickname "Chris." Light complexion acne. Greenish-blue eyes. Brown hair. Dyed blond, waist length. Curved scar left heel. Faint birth mark right front thigh. Vaccination scar left upper arm. Two teeth short in lower jaw, never developed. Likes rock music, hippie-type headbands and leather neck strap. "Please darling call me, we love you, will send you money." Grandma. Contact: Mr & Mrs James Sanderson, 216 So. Putnam, Pueblo, Colorado . . .

Or does it mean this?

disclosures that between five and ten per cent of the 62,000 school-children in Omaha, Nebraska, are taking the 'behaviour modification' drugs Ritalin, dexedrene, aventyl and tofranil prescribed by doctors to improve their classroom behaviour, have started a storm in the city . . . Dr Byron Oberst, an Omaha pediatrician, was instrumental in introducing the 'behaviour modification' programme to the municipal schools just over a year ago. Now some children in nearly all the city's schools are on the drugs . . . The drugs are being given to pupils regarded as 'hyperactive' and unmanageable.

Or does it mean something else altogether? Something that is neither the excruciatingly detailed description of a missing child given to the *National Missing Youth Locator*[21] for posting in 10,000 police departments, sheriff's offices and social agencies across America, nor the extension of the conventional treatments of the insane asylum into the field of education that the Omaha "experiment"[22] represents. Does it mean the scientific analysis of Dr. Bronfenbrenner?[23]

As we read the evidence, both from our own research and that of others, we cannot escape the conclusion that, if the current trend persists, if the institutions of our society continue to remove parents, other adults, and older youth from active participation in the lives of children, and if the resulting vacuum is filled by the age-segregated peer group, *we can look forward to increased alienation, indifference, antagonism and violence on the part of the younger generation in all segments of our society.*

Or does it mean the wild guessing of novelist Marya Mannes[24] —which in any case corroborates Bronfenbrenner's "research."

[21] The NMYL is (1971) a private organization which circulates photographs and descriptions of runaways for concerned parents prepared to pay between twenty and thirty dollars per insertion per week (*Rolling Stone,* February 4, 1971).

[22] Extract from report in London *Daily Telegraph,* June 6, 1970.

[23] Bronfenbrenner, *op. cit.*

[24] Marya Mannes, *They* (Doubleday, New York, 1968). The novel deals with "a nightmarish totalitarian America ruled by teenagers."

We are producing a breed of spiritual illiterates, people without self-control and with only one goal in life—to get what they want regardless of anyone else, and to get it now. People who think freedom means the instant gratification of desire—*their* desire —and are forgiven everything because they are young.

In fact it does not matter what "caring" really is. The important thing is that it is now something that must be proved to be something else to the half-million American teenagers who leave home every year and do not wish to be tracked down like criminals as a result. In Britain, a country cited by Bronfenbrenner as the only one of six, East and West, where "antisocial" behavior among children is more pronounced than in the United States, a 1972 survey of attitudes among secondary-school children revealed that two-thirds of the sample passionately objected to "adults lying about young people, searching their private possessions, spying on them, listening to their telephone calls and being 'over-familiar.' "[25] The kids have said no to "caring"; they prefer "lowered social capacity" instead.

Thus we see in parental attitudes to children the same guilty complicity lurking beneath a camouflage of outrage as we have seen adopted by cornered administrators in earlier examples. In marriage the child, either unwanted or wanted for unrealistic reasons, rapidly develops into an impediment to the personal lives of husband and wife. As a result the husband concentrates on his career, his car, his stereo system or whatever, while the wife assumes increased burdens which she either suffers in bitterness or contrives to lighten by adopting an analysis of her situation which clarifies her very real exploited status. The child does not escape: either it spends all its time with one adult person—which is limiting and exhausting for both—or it begins to develop a life outside the home which

---

[25] Report of the Schools Council Project in Moral Education: *Moral Education in the Secondary School* (Longman, London, 1972).

sooner or later it will be accused of doing as an act of treach-
ery and ingratitude. As the child approaches maturity the
parental crisis escalates into its definitive phase, where the
guilt of the husband encounters the bitterness of the wife. An
explanation becomes urgently necessary, and is provided by
the "irresponsibility" and "ingratitude" of the child which, in
its natural desire to escape such accusations, leaves home and
thus closes the door on the fruitless episode of its youth. There-
upon fifteen to eighteen years of duty and obligation explode
into a comprehensive denunciation of the behavior of young
people in general and relations between the protagonists dissolve. Not into an acknowledgment of the separate aspirations
of each, but as with the anger of the citizens of Fresno and the
exasperation of the Criminal Law Revision Committee, into a
vengeful and irrational distribution of blame. The child blames
the parents, the parents blame the child and each other, all
according to well-known stereotypes. The result is militancy
on all sides: the child resolves to avoid the pattern of life of
its parents, the wife sees her marriage as a trap into which she
stupidly wandered at an early age, the husband—who probably did best out of the whole deal—resolves too late to make
it up to his wife and takes it out on kids everywhere. Thus
the several causes of counter-culture revolt, women's liberation,
male chauvinism and punitive social control are simultaneously
served by a repetitive and atomizing pattern of life.

The social result of this popular melodrama, piously denounced as "lowered social capacity," is to be clearly seen in
two apparently contradictory developments. On one side, the
proliferation of social theorists, revolutionaries, counselors,
social workers, psychiatrists, teachers and law enforcement
officers who busily erect monstrous theoretical and administrative structures to take over the abandoned parental function.
On the other the growing demand for technical and legal means
to avoid such dismal crises in the future. Contraceptive devices,
liberalized divorce and abortion laws, unalienable property

rights for husband and wife, more single-person accommodation, more labor-saving devices. There is no contradiction really, because "lowered social capacity" is both the lesson of family life and the antithesis of parental *care*. It is what is learned and what is desired, not a disease but a cure in itself.

Just as the small suburban house and its attendant life-style represented a means of escape from the system of community obligations so nostalgically recalled by Bronfenbrenner, so is it also the incubator of an even more fragmentary and microscopic social unit which will eventually succeed it. The private individual, traumatized survivor of the nuclear family explosion, will in his turn escape from his fruitless past, taking with him the lessons he has learned from a generational experience of scapegoatism, caricature, legal and social regression, osstensibility and—most important and predictive of all—a knowledge of the selfless and magical service of machines.

CHAPTER FOUR

ENVIRONMENTAL TERRORISM

The January 1973 issue of the journal of the American Association for the Advancement of Science contained an account by Dr. David L. Rosenhan, professor of psychology and law at Stanford University, of two experiments, carried out the preceding year, to determine whether psychiatric hospitals could in fact determine the difference between the sane and the insane. In the course of the first experiment three psychologists, a pediatrician, a psychiatrist, a painter and a housewife simulated insanity in order to be admitted to mental hospitals. Their efforts were uniformly successful, in fact more than one of them gained access to more than one hospital, a total of twelve in five states, East and West, being involved.

The pseudopatients all told the same story—that they repeatedly heard strange voices saying "empty," "hollow" and "thud." Otherwise they told the truth about themselves, including relationships with family and friends. Once inside the pseudopatients stopped faking their symptom. They spoke to patients and staff members as they normally would to anyone. They accepted medication but flushed it down a toilet—as they saw other patients doing also. All told, they were given nearly 2,100 pills, mostly tranquilizers. When asked how they felt, they said "fine"—their symptoms had disappeared.

Since there was little to do in the wards all the pseudo-patients took copious notes of what was happening. At first they hid their note-taking but soon saw that no one cared and did it openly. Some patients began to voice suspicions about them. "You're not crazy. You're a journalist or a professor. You're checking up on the hospital." But the hospital staffs never questioned the regular note-taking. One nurse saw it as a symptom of a compulsion. "Patient engages in writing behavior," she wrote on his chart day after day.

The pseudopatients experiment was not detected at any one of the twelve hospitals. Each was discharged with a diagnosis of schizophrenia "in remission." The length of hospital stays ranged from seven to fifty-two days.

To see if the tendency towards diagnosing the sane as insane could be reversed, Dr. Rosenhan carried out a second experiment involving the staff at a research and teaching hospital who had heard and disbelieved the results of the first. They were told that at some time in the next three months one or more pseudopatients would seek admittance to their hospital. Each staff member was therefore on his guard to detect any pseudopatient.

The staff members recorded their opinions about 193 admissions during the trial period. Forty-one were said to be pseudo-patients by at least one staff member. Twenty-three were considered "suspect" by at least one psychiatrist. During the trial period Dr. Rosenhan had not sent a single pseudopatient to the hospital.[1]

In 1967 several British newspapers carried stories about a

[1] Account taken from *The New York Times,* January 21, 1973.

"metric street numbering system" which had been experimentally employed in the town of Dudley in Worcestershire.[2] Instead of having 1, 3, 5 on one side and 2, 4, 6 on the other, houses were numbered by the distance in metres between their front gates. The first was number one. If the next was fifteen metres further on it became sixteen. Officials paced out the distances between houses up one side of the street and then down the other. According to the newspapers, plans to extend the system had been abandoned after an outcry from families whose visitors got lost, from bewildered postmen who were obliged to convert old numbers to new by means of "an expensive list," and from doctors who could not find homes during emergency calls.

Six months before the incident of the "metric numbering system" a popular British newspaper carried a small news item about a sixty-eight-year-old widow who had lived in her bathroom for a month because gas board engineers converting appliances from town to natural gas had disconnected her two gas heaters.[3] As the bathroom was the only electrically heated room in her house she had moved in there, enduring great discomfort, until in desperation she had written a letter to the Queen. Surprisingly this mediaeval remedy resulted in a speedy reconnection to the gas supply. Some time later another newspaper reported the distress of the parents of an eleven-year-old girl who had been killed by a runaway driverless bus belonging to the Midland Red bus company, the largest in Britain. The bus company offered no condolences over their tragic loss even though a subsequent safety check on their vehicles had resulted in thirty-two of them being declared unsafe pending mechanical repairs. The general manager of the company explained to a journalist that insurance complications made it inadvisable for them to make any gesture apart from

[2] "Metric Numbers Lead Postmen up the Garden Path," *Sunday Express,* June 7, 1970.
[3] "Woman Lived in Her Bathroom for a Month," *Daily Mirror,* February 20, 1970.

the formal expression of regret voiced by their counsel at the inquest.[4]

In 1971, as a result of rising unemployment in Britain, much media discussion focused on the workings of the welfare services. A Sunday newspaper discovered the existence of an administrative device known as the "wage-stop," apparently instituted some time in 1968, which achieved the goal of maintaining the claimant's enthusiasm for work by cutting the benefit to which he was entitled to a figure just below the recorded earnings for his last job.[5] In August 1971 it was estimated that 100,000 people received benefit subject to this proviso. Further revelations were made concerning the growing army of special investigators operated by the Ministry of Social Security as means to cut down instances of embezzlement. One of the principal duties of these people, it transpired, was to investigate reported cases of cohabitation among the 200,000 women wholly or partly dependent on social-security benefits. These special investigators, whose salaries amounted to £1,000,000 per year, had allegedly saved the department £900,000 by exposing cases of cohabitation. An independent report submitted to the Fisher Committee on social-security abuse showed that of twenty cases investigated, only one revealed any evidence of financial support from the man suspected of cohabiting.[6]

The second annual report of the Parliamentary Commissioner for Administration (Ombudsman), 1972, revealed that of 182 complaints investigated, the majority related to the Inland Revenue Service. One example told of income-tax demands which plagued the widow of a man who had died in

---

[4] "Bus Firm 'Showed No Pity' After Girl Was Killed," *Sunday Express,* April 4, 1972.
[5] "The Secret Machinery of the Poverty Code," The London *Sunday Times,* August 8, 1971.
[6] "Sex Inquiries Turning Women into Prostitutes," the London *Times,* April 14, 1972.

October 1970 despite repeated communications from her explaining the situation.[7] Six months after his death a threat to
levy distraint drove the widow to seek the aid of her member
of parliament.

In 1972 a London newspaper revealed that, acting under
the instructions of a number of Home Office circulars, police
forces throughout Britain notified professional, trade and
government associations whenever any of their members
committed an offense against the law, even if no conviction
followed.[8] Civil servants, nurses, dentists, doctors, solicitors,
teachers, public-service vehicle drivers and conductors, as well
as postmen, all faced an automatic reporting procedure should
they fall foul of the police. A few months earlier another newspaper reported proposals by HM Chief Inspector of Constabu-
lary for the future development of the policeman's role in
society. He suggested that each small community might set
up a "mini crime prevention committee" consisting of the headmaster of the local school, church leaders, youth leaders and
the parks foreman to work in conjunction with the police on
the basis of pooled information. Traffic wardens too would
have a role in this arrangement acting as "the eyes and ears of
the police."[9]

In the summer of 1971 several British newspapers carried
the story of a young mother, Mrs. Elizabeth Nuttall, who had
delivered her own baby in a council flat on the twentieth floor
of a London tower block.[10] She and her husband and one other
child had moved into the flat from a slum area one month
before, they had no telephone and the husband worked nights,

---

[7] "Beyond the Grave Chase by Taxman," *Evening Standard,* February 24,
1972.

[8] "Police Files for Private Courts," the London *Sunday Times,* June 11,
1972.

[9] "Traffic Wardens Could Help Police More," Manchester *Guardian,* September 29, 1971.

[10] " 'Too Shy' Elizabeth Delivers Her Own Baby," the London *Daily Mail,*
July 3, 1971.

they knew none of their neighbors and none responded to her screams for help. On arrival in the block they had been given a card with the addresses of neighboring churches, shops and public houses; but no information about doctors. Even after the successful delivery she had to walk two miles before she could find a public telephone in working order.

The following month a popular Sunday newspaper reported that an old couple living in state-subsidized housing had been threatened with eviction because the housing manager had discovered that their grandchildren had come to stay with them for a holiday. "If they couldn't have afforded a hotel room they shouldn't have let the children come," he said.[11] In the same week another newspaper reported that thirty-two families in subsidized housing had complained because bull-dozers had ripped through their gardens to begin a new estate. The tenants had been given twenty-four hours' notice.[12] A year earlier another newspaper had reported the eviction by fifty police of a family of seven from a London council maisonette. The family, including a handicapped daughter, resisted be-cause the alternative accommodation offered them had no garden.[13] In a letter to *The New York Times* protesting about suburban resistance to public housing, the chairman of the New York City Housing Authority defended the crime record of public housing in terms appropriate to both sides of the Atlantic.[14]

The simple fact is that public housing, far from causing crime, is one of the most effective deterrents to crime. The rate of crime in public housing is one-third that of the city as a whole. The reason

[11] "Council Rules: Kick out Children," the London *News of the World,* August 22, 1971.
[12] "Old People in Tears as Gardens Ploughed Up," the London *Daily Mirror,* August 16, 1971.
[13] "Battle as Police Win Home Siege," *The Sun,* May 8, 1970.
[14] "Simeon Golar Discusses Forest Hills," *The New York Times,* January 12, 1972.

is simple—public housing tenants are by and large the working poor. They are carefully selected and subject to eviction if they show evidence of antisocial behavior. Further, the Authority has its own police force of over 1,500 men who patrol the projects in addition to the normal city police coverage available to everyone else.

Concern over inflated property prices during 1971 and 1972 led to many newspaper and magazine articles covering the effects on those unable or unwilling to buy as well as those whose attempts to purchase were continually thwarted. A man who had agreed to a purchase price of £12,500 for a London flat was told three days later that the price had risen to £12,750. When this price was agreed to in writing the owner's agents had again raised it to £13,750. Reluctantly the purchaser agreed to the new price and despatched a ten per cent deposit. This was returned immediately by the owner's agents with the news that "an administrative error" had led to the agreement on the previous price, in fact the purchase price should have been in the region of £18,000. The purchaser abandoned his efforts at this point,[15] but others were more persistent. One month before in St. John's Wood, London, would-be purchasers of flats priced up to £32,000 lined up for four days, living in cars and under canvas and fighting off intruders who tried to muscle in at the head of the line.[16] In 1971 a retired engineer shot the married couple living next to him because they had come to live in a house built next to the isolated bungalow he had occupied for twelve years.[17] House prices in some areas of London rose by over 40 per cent during 1971.

---

[15] "Landlords Offering Tenants Thousands of Pounds to Quit," the London *Times*, April 8, 1972.
[16] *Ibid.*
[17] "Double Murder and a Suicide—in Feud over Garden," *Daily Mail*, August 4, 1971.

A report to the government by the French Medical Council in 1971 showed that almost sixty per cent of all the admissions to French mental institutions could be traced to the harassing effect of noise. Experiments carried out at the Chelsea College of Science and Technology in the same year showed that infrasound—low-frequency vibrations once tested by the German army for their weapons potential, and later developed by the French into a system capable of vibrating enemy soldiers to death at a range of five miles—affected motorists under normal driving conditions. The symptoms included a kind of drunkenness as well as a 30 per cent reduction in peripheral vision.[18] British experiments into aircraft noise revealed that persons living in the vicinity of airports were eight times more likely to seek medical aid for psychological disorders than the national average. Ecologists, whose threats of doom through population growth, accelerating pollution and the exhaustion of world resources enjoyed an unprecedented vogue during the early nineteen-seventies, frequently quoted the case of the James Island deer. Five Sika deer had been released on the half-square-mile uninhabited island in Chesapeake Bay in 1916. By 1956 the herd had increased to 300 but stress induced by overcrowding caused half of them to die in 1958 and the population to level off at about eighty the year after.[19] Extrapolating vigorously, one best-selling author concluded that, the deer having started to die at a density of one every eighty yards, the human prognosis for stress conditions could be expected to reach catastrophe between the years 2000 and 2070, when the distribution of world population would place humans at intervals of 120 yards and 60 yards respectively.

Readers of *The New York Times* in 1971 learned that each Sunday edition of their paper consumed two hundred acres of

[18] "Noise! It Can Drive You Insane," the London *Sunday Mirror*, September 24, 1972.
[19] Gordon Rattray Taylor, *The Doomsday Book* (Thames and Hudson, London, 1970).

fully grown forest. Watchers on television learned that two acres of open country are consumed every minute by buildings and cars. Airline passengers learned from their inflight magazines that civil aircraft all over the world burned 3,000 tons of precious oxygen every ten minutes. They also learned, from other sources, that in the first quarter of 1972 eight hundred persons had been arrested as a result of efforts to screen out potential hijackers at American airports. A further 2,000 had been refused boarding passes because they conformed to a "behavioral profile pattern" built up from a study of previous hijackers. Aircraft hijackings over the preceding seventeen years, had, according to the Airline Pilots' Association, already caused the deaths of 400 passengers and 50 crewmen, as well as the destruction of 50 million dollars' worth of aircraft. New York car drivers learned that their vehicles emitted 1,500 tons of carbon monoxide gas every day. Swedish mothers were told that the milk in their breasts contained 70 per cent more DDT than would be permitted in artificial varieties.[20] In the spring of 1972 an English newspaper columnist produced an amusing piece similar to the students' magazine example cited at the beginning of this chapter[21] explaining that the government had published a white paper announcing "radical changes in the English language." The government's proposals, he wrote, were complex and far-reaching but in effect they meant that by 1975 "we will all be speaking Japanese." *Time* magazine for April 17, 1972 carried a story about a ten-year-old boy who earned pocket money by carrying shopping to customers' cars from a supermarket in Chicago. Passing by an armored truck awaiting the day's takings from the supermarket, he was shot dead by a guard who said he had been harassed by teenagers.

---

[20] *Ibid.*

[21] Keith Waterhouse, "Getting in Line," the London *Daily Mirror,* February 18, 1972.

These incidents, statements and examples have been quoted at some length only to give an impression of the enormous volume of terrifying, worrying, incomprehensible and depressing items that go into the ordinary information input of any Western citizen. Quite apart from anxieties derived from headline news and the compulsive threats and cajolery of advertising itself, the ordinary newspaper reader finds between the front page and the sports pages innumerable items of the kind listed above. In Britain alone there are between five and six million families living in subsidized public housing for whom every tale of bureaucratic high-handedness, summary eviction and increased surveillance has a direct, personal meaning. There are four or five million mortgage-holders who view rising interest rates and galloping prices with mixed feelings, perhaps another two million would-be purchasers who read with sinking hearts of prices rising steadily above any conceivable amortization of their own earning capacity. Certainly millions of airline passengers take their seats with increasing trepidation. All over the Western world a morning newspaper, an evening of television, a weekend magazine—all convey images of intolerable impermanence and ever-present danger. Mass media make doomsday more than a private moral fate, instead it has become a measurable, predictable public death. The aggregate environmental effect of millions of private cars has become a better index of the perniciousness of their owners than any prediction of disaster based on individual improvidence, greed or laziness. All consumers have become not so much moral sinners as ecological criminals, contributing to the destruction of the *whole world* through their own individual thoughtless extravagance. For the second time in the history of the modern world the day of judgment has been quantified, measured and assigned a date—according to the Club of Rome study *The Limits to Growth,* it may be expected in the second decade of the next century.

The world horror image of press, TV, magazine, book and

film is not merely a figment of the media mirror, it is real too. That is why the sort of stories quoted above are much more effective than the bed-hopping of international foreign policy or the crises of sport. Persons who could pass by a man carrying a placard predicting divine intervention with a gay laugh, wipe the grins off their faces when they come across a traffic policeman sucking oxygen, or a river boiling with "cooling" water from some industrial facility. This, it is widely believed, is the real thing. One of three "real things" standing in the newspaper offices of the world, each ready to seize the headline should the occasion serve. Moral doomsday is one, the fate of Sodom and Gomorrah lately brought up to date by emphasis on "anarchy," "terrorism" and the endless ramifications of drug abuse. Nuclear holocaust is another, always ready to make an entrance in the event of tricky international negotiations or excessive *gung ho* on the part of air force generals. Ecological catastrophe is the third, at present riding high on computerized calculations involving round figures of enormous magnitude.[22] Beyond them are the masses of minor tales all contributing to the pervasive sense of vulnerability that is a dominant characteristic of our much-prized "security." "News" is an important part of the pattern of *environmental terrorism* that feeds the rewarding circle of withdrawal from the public realm.

Environmental terrorism is an all-embracing phenomenon; it informs the meaning of all that is perceived. It is an integral part of the behavioral structure of any consumer society. Just as the development and proliferation of consumer goods draws the individual deeper and deeper into a technologically reinforced nirvana of private satisfactions, so does environmental terrorism—or "news" of the disasters that befall other people —push him determinedly in the same direction. There is no

---

[22] Reputedly each day of the 1972 United Nations conference on the environment held in Stockholm began with the distribution of *three tons* of information material.

escape from it through electronic communication because the cheapest transistor set and the smallest portable TV will smuggle it into the most remote retreat, even into the automobile itself. This is no accident; the endless reinforcement of the decision of withdrawal is a vital part of its mechanism. It serves the same purpose as atrocity propaganda during a war: the worse you believe the enemy to be, the less likely you are to let them get their hands on you. The self-administered propaganda of "news" is a maintenance dose of aversion therapy.

This interlocking process of consumer goods pull and news media push has the character of a syndrome in that it gains power with each successive cycle. The privatized individual vacates the public realm which thus falls progressively into the hands of a bureaucracy laced with speculative corruption. Such administration in turn leads to more news of families evicted and old ladies living in their bathrooms and thus confirms the wisdom of the initial withdrawal itself. Because the public realm is less and less often *experienced* and more and more *reported* it becomes an image consisting of rapes, hijackings, riots, speeches, murders and rackets. Standards of public life fall—or so it appears—and the apparent fall acts as an additional confirmation of its dangers. What else can you expect from public life? Better by far to keep out of it, or vicariously endure its cycles of violence and duplicity on TV.

Once the syndrome has begun, draconian legislation to restrict the exercise of public rights of action inevitably follows. Implementation of this legislation generates protest, protest leads to more televised and reported acts of violence and the violence in turn confirms the necessity of the legislation as well as the need for more. The fear of the privatized citizen is continually reinforced, and with it his desire to strengthen the walls of his own privacy by dissociating himself from any remaining strands of obligation that still reach out into the public arena from his home or his job.

Because the process of social withdrawal is self-reinforcing, attempts to combat it by diverting resources into decaying community structures are ultimately self-defeating. Worse still, they tend to increase the scope of arbitrary and unjust administration and thus make the specter of environmental terrorism loom larger still. The consequences of privatization for the individual who attains it include, as we have seen, a steady reduction in the number of persons among whom he lives and for whom he accepts any responsibility, as well as a countervailing increase in the number of mechanisms or inanimate energy slaves he requires to sustain his isolation. This simultaneous process of depopulation and systematization has direct effects upon the post-communal organization of public life. Within the breakdown of community structure and its replacement by a centralized servicing system occurs a parallel reorganization of the physical pattern of administration and supply. Interlocking circles are replaced by radiating lines and the effect is much the same as that which has been observed in recent years in the decline of the railroads and their supersession by motorways and private cars. Vast areas of accommodation fall vacant, reservoirs of demand and employment dry up, new and different utilizations take their places.

Like unprofitable railroads which can only be kept running with massive subsidies, collapsed communities are attended by increasing numbers of social workers who are paid to prop up a structure collapsing of its own weight. If parents have ceased to care about their children, social workers will do it for them. If the children in turn have ceased to support their parents in old age, welfare will assume the burden. The old patterns of community care are patched up repeatedly by infusions of public money and professional skill. The result, however, is not a real strengthening of the bonds of community obligation, any more than the result of railroad subsidy is a renewed ability to make a profit. On the contrary, the labor of social workers merely reinforces the desire of their charges to withdraw from responsibilities which have long ceased to correspond to any recognizable personal goals.

This logical but unpalatable state of affairs can be clearly observed in the writings of those involved in efforts to revitalize the depressed areas of Western cities. The attempts of social and housing aid agencies to repair the damage consumer longings have done to the ancient combination of resignation and mutual obligation which made poverty look after itself are doomed to failure—if only because the one thing they cannot offer is the private prosperity that is craved. This failure is expressed in the endless extension of bureaucratic power over the non-affluent, and a corresponding extension in the pattern of environmental terrorism which spurs those better off to avoid their fate at all costs. The director of a volunteer neighborhood action project in Liverpool offered this summation in 1971:

Unemployment benefit sustains a man temporarily, but if his unemployment problem is also the school problem, the health, housing, poverty and race problem, then that benefit is neither remedial, structural, nor adequate. *Studied in depth, even public intervention can become a means of negative discrimination. The most conscientious officers can have a dehumanizing effect on the poor . . .*
Housing has little to do with arbitrary standards inherited from medical and engineering traditions. *It has everything to do with who occupies it—or, more precisely, with whether the occupants are winning or losing in their search for wealth, or power, or prestige . . .*
All social legislation (including housing Acts and planning Acts) is useful only to the extent that it facilitates mobility. In so far as housing and physical planning strategies, and the whole range of welfare benefits, subsidies, and social services, *do not structurally combine to alter the prospects of the trapped urban poor,* then we remain advocates who treat symptoms rather than disease.[23]

The italics are not those of the author of the article, princi-

[23] Des McConaghy, "The Limitations of Advocacy," *Royal Institute of British Architects Journal,* February 1972.

pally because he—in common with most dedicated workers in the field—still sees these factors as difficulties with which social workers must contend, rather than structural defects which make their work ultimately self-defeating. If the talisman of successful social work is the ability to facilitate "winning" in the search for wealth, then it becomes difficult to distinguish between social work and public lottery, or indeed social work and crime—which is in one sense the purest expression of the private pursuit of wealth.[24] The supportive administrative system offered by the social worker is not what is desired by the occupant of the depressed urban area; what he wants is a chance to catch up with those less poor than himself. When he divines that there is no real aid to be expected from the welfare bureaucracy in this direction, he sees them instead as a positive hindrance to any chances of wealth he might still possess. And he is right to do so. The growth and proliferation of social-security benefit systems amounts to a trap. Once enmeshed in it the poor family rapidly loses the ability to escape.

In Britain there are now nearly fifty national means tests which determine eligibility for subsidies or exemption from charges, and a further 3,000 operated by local authorities all over the country. In many cases their operation amounts to an unintentional but severe tax on low wage earners, dependents and the unemployed. For example, a man earning £19 a week with a wife and two children will become eligible for a family income supplement. But if he then increases his wages by an extra pound a week, he will lose £1.44 in benefits and income tax, leaving him worse off than before. He would lose 50p in

---

[24] Harold D. Lasswell and Jeremiah McKenna's 1970 report on Brooklyn's Bedford-Stuyvesant district indicated that the black population of the area spent $88,000,000 on drugs and gambling in that year—about $11,000,000 more than it collected in welfare payments. The numbers operation alone had an annual payroll of $15,000,000, making it the biggest private employer in the area. "There is community support for some crime because it delivers vital services," suggests Professor Francis Ianni of Columbia University in "The Irregular Economy," *Time,* February 19, 1973.

family income supplement, 60p for free school meals for his children, 30p in income tax and 4 p in higher national insurance contributions. Rent rebate schemes governing his subsidized housing will drop by another 17p, bringing his total loss to £1.61 as a result of increasing his income by an extra one pound a week. If he should become unemployed the wage stop mentioned above will hold his welfare payments down to a level below £19 per week.[25]

How is a wage-earner enmeshed in such a system of contradictions to begin to realize his dream of a house of his own, a car of his own, a color television, a foreign holiday? The answer is that he is not able to. In accepting social security he has hopelessly enmeshed himself in a bureaucratic network of surveillance and obligation more onerous by far than the old family structure that his yearnings for affluence have already caused him to break up. How is a wage-earner enmeshed in this system to be expected to regard his tormentors—half-trained, half-educated, pompous functionaries—as anything more than reminders of the paternalistic slavery he wishes so desperately to flee? The answer is that he is not. When they employ special investigators to catch people who are receiving benefits to which they claim the recipients are not entitled, when they deport people to re-establishment centers and rehabilitation centers, when they separate husbands and wives by sending men to jobs on the other side of the country, there can be no question of regarding them as anything but oppressors.

It is in this way that the pursuit of privatization, even among those who cannot attain it, confirms the collapse of community. The armies of social workers, the endless talk of participation, community democracy, decentralization of government power, neighborhood councils and so on, all make no difference in the end—or rather they make one difference. The

---

[25] This example was taken from a social-welfare survey carried out by the London *Times,* March 8, 1972.

network of legislation, surveillance, petty tyranny and exploitation that social-welfare programs visit upon those they profess to help sends vibrations up the social ladder and across the divide between the haves and the have nots. As inflation, reduced economic growth and unemployment bring the threshold of social welfare nearer, those threatened by it make energetic, even frenzied, efforts to divest themselves of all involvement with the welfare legislation that was popularly voted into existence a bare quarter of a century ago.

The British National Health Service, a system of free medical care paid for out of deductions from earnings which was instituted in 1948, is today seriously threatened by the rapid growth of private health insurance schemes. In 1948 there were only 54,000 subscribers to private health insurance, in 1960 447,000, in 1969 nearly a million, and in 1972 two million. An Institute of Economic Affairs public-opinion poll carried out in 1970 indicated that 71 per cent of the population opposed increased payments for not ony medical services but also retirement pensions and education. 70 per cent were in favor of reducing payments on all three to a level where only those "in real need" would be covered. The remainder would contract out of all the major state systems in favor of private enterprise.[26]

More extreme even than this energetic rejection of the mechanism of collective responsibility has been the parallel perversion of what was once an egalitarian social housing policy into a nationwide organization for the promotion of private ownership. Since owner occupation, like automobile ownership, represents one of the key resources of privatization, this process deserves description at greater length.

---

[26] *Choice in Welfare 1970* (Institute of Economic Affairs, London, 1971). There is evidence that the same attitude dominates in the U.S.A. A reader survey on guaranteed minimum income carried out by the *National Inquirer* (March 1973) showed 87.4 per cent opposed to the introduction of a federal wage supplement.

Although some considerable public health legislation affecting housing was passed in Britain during the nineteenth century, very little housing was constructed using public funds prior to the First World War. In 1914 well over 80 per cent of the eight million dwellings in England and Wales were rented to private tenants by private landlords, and this was the norm for working-class housing all over Europe. Housing was built according to market forces and market returns, and even the housing built by charities such as the Peabody and Waterlow trusts was intended to show a 6 per cent profit. This situation changed drastically shortly after the outbreak of war, when the manpower demands of the services and war industries stimulated housing demand at the same time as shortages of materials and labor put an end to new construction. As a result, a fierce inflation in rents and house prices began which within a year threatened civil unrest on a scale unacceptable to any wartime government. Rents were therefore stabilized at 1914 figures by government decree, with the result that by 1918 there could be no question of a return to a free market for fear of a catastrophic rise in costs. In consequence legislation was passed in 1919 to empower local administrations all over the country to assess housing need and respond to it by constructing dwellings to be let at heavily subsidized rents. Approximately one million dwellings were constructed according to this formula by the outbreak of the Second World War in 1939. During the same period private builders completed three times as many houses, most of them for sale to owner occupiers, so that by 1939 the proportion of privately rented accommodation had sunk to about 55 per cent of the total while that of privately owned property had risen to about 35 per cent. Rent controls had been retained, with some minor revision, throughout the interwar period, with the result that private building for rental had virtually ceased except in the case of apartment blocks in large cities.

The effect of the Second World War was similar to that of

the First except that aerial bombardment had caused the destruction of half a million houses. By 1945 the gross shortage was in the region of two million dwellings and the incoming socialist administration resolved to overcome it by concentrating on the construction of subsidized housing according to the principles established before the war. Housing was to be provided as a social service, like medicine and education, and the principal agency was to be the local authority. The private sector was effectively muzzled by a system of licensing and a 100 per cent development levy guaranteed that private fortunes would not be made out of state-licensed reconstruction. This drastic program failed to realize the extravagant hopes pinned on it. Six years of public housing in conditions of postwar austerity and exhaustion failed even to equal the rates of construction achieved by private builders alone a decade before. With the fall of the socialist administration in 1951, emphasis returned to the private sector, where it has remained ever since. For a time parity between public and private sectors was maintained in terms of the annual number of completions, but the steady growth of the building societies, the nonprofit organizations which financed the vast majority of house purchases, bore witness to a gathering enthusiasm for owner occupation. The Labour party rapidly abandoned their earlier goal of housing as a social service and from 1959 onward the goal of a property-owning democracy was shared by both major parties. Direct encouragement of owner occupation by means of taxation relief and the abandonment of property tax facilitated a steady increase in house prices.

By the close of the 1960's it had become evident that the average owner occupier moved house every six or seven years in the same way as he traded in his car every two or three years. Ownership had become less a matter of territoriality than of successful financial speculation. The consequences of this situation for those not yet on the first rung of the ladder of purchase were clearly grave. Calculations showed that between

1964 and 1969 the increase in the price of houses, unmatched by an equivalent increase in incomes, had effectively disenfranchised half those who could have afforded to buy a house in the former year. Nonetheless the percentage of owner-occupied dwellings had increased in fifty years by two and a half times.

The inflationary grasp of owner occupation had its effect on public housing as well. Letting 30 per cent of the accommodation in the country at subsidized rents—a quarter of them under £1 per week as late as 1970—local-authority building obviously could not be financed on the basis of rent income. It was never intended to be. Nonetheless the escalating cost of land attributable to real and artificial scarcity—the latter created by zoning regulations—affected the abilities of local authorities, particularly those in urban areas where, as we have seen, the majority of the population dwells, to purchase on the open market. Exchequer loan subsidies to local authorities rose dramatically during the sixties until it became evident that the battle with profitable commercial interests and well-financed owner occupiers could never be won. In London, for example, where the inner boroughs were committed to housing an indigenous population impoverished by the banishment of industry[27] on some of the most expensive land in the world, the rents they were able to charge (and the low densities at which they were compelled to build) were so small in relation to the real cost of demolition and renewal, that their loan repayments began to equal or even exceed the sums available to finance new building. They were borrowing money to repay money they had already borrowed rather than to build anew. The 100 per cent development levy imposed by the socialists had been abandoned by their successors so that indirectly the success of the private market was conspiring to ruin the public sector as rent control had ruined the private landlord.

---

[27] Planning estimates in 1972 indicated that London is losing jobs at the rate of 10,000 a year owing to industrial relocation.

Inevitably some means of increasing the rents for public-sector properties had to be devised—either that, or some control of the price of land. The latter course was ruled out by the interests of the powerful owner-occupier lobby. Over 50 per cent of the housing in the country was now privately owned, and those owners constituted a political force with every interest in maintaining the status quo. With their houses increasing in value by up to 40 per cent in a single year, they saw scarcity and demand as positive forces which augmented their own personal wealth. The methods chosen were the *earnings-related* subsidy and the sale of public housing. In effect the public sector was to be squeezed to feed the private sector. Faced with heavy rent increases, the public-sector tenant could either pay up according to his income—with results that we have already described—or buy in, either on the open market or through his local authority which became increasingly prepared to sell him the house in which he lived as a means to restore its own housing revenue account to credit. Eventually the ironically named "fair-rent" system was extended to cover the vestigial private-rental sector so that it too could be squeezed to feed the owner-occupier market.

Even before this legislation took effect in the autumn of 1972, its consequences could be clearly seen in an unprecedented rush to buy. House prices in the London area rose by 12 per cent in the first six months of 1971, by a further 15 per cent in the second half of the year, and a further 15 per cent in the first quarter of 1972. The consequences for potential purchasers, as the examples given earlier in this chapter show, became catastrophic. On present trends a home which cost £10,-000 in 1970 must be worth £20,000 by 1980. Similarly, because of rising labor costs, a home which costs £10,000 to build today will cost £20,000 to build in ten years' time. If you do not buy today you must double your income within a decade if you are to think of buying tomorrow.

Clearly the triumph of the housing policy of the owner occupier—there is no other way to describe the manipulation of the economics of half the housing in England and Wales to feed the demand generated by the other half—represents the triumph of privatization in an important area of social administration. Like the well-mounted attacks on the health service described earlier, like the attacks on state pensions and even the education system itself, it shows the extraordinary power of private desires when translated into public policy. At the same time it reveals the mechanism whereby the vacated area of public responsibility is first made unworkable, then drastically altered so that its original purpose as a social service is lost, and finally frankly recognized as a servicing and support system for the private sector—a system, moreover, which is licensed to practice environmental terrorism in its most literal form on those unable to escape the public sector for the haven of ownership and affluence.[28]

As we have seen, the development and proliferation of a social bureaucracy intended to patch up the ravages of private interests in no way mitigates the collapse of community. The rule of that bureaucracy, no matter how well-intentioned, amounts to a system of terror that threatens its victims in such a way that the instant acquisition of wealth becomes the only possible means of escape. In Britain thirteen different types of social worker (truant officer, school care committee, psychiatric social worker, probation officer, children's department, Family Welfare Association, housing social worker, health visi-

---

[28] The vicar of a parish church in the London district of Hackney wrote in his parish magazine in July 1972 that increased reliance on drink and drugs were signs of fear in the population. ". . . Who knows how much longer some of us will be allowed to live in our present homes? Which street will be requisitioned next? Where will we be shuffled off to when the time eventually comes to pull down our street to make way for the next expensive, badly-built and ill-planned housing conglomeration? Those who live in new houses and flats can hardly tell when the next rent increase will be thrust upon them, or if their jobs are really secure. And shall any of us—let alone poor pensioners—be able indefinitely to cope with inflation and rising prices?"

tor, home help organizer, medical social worker, family service unit, National Society for the Prevention of Cruelty to Children, Ministry of Social Security) can be involved in the predicament of a single family. In the sense of helping to meet the *desires* of that family—as opposed to what are interpreted as its *needs*—not one of them can be as useful as a win on the football pools, an unforeseen legacy, a good bet on the horses, or even a lucky day at bingo.

In Britain in 1972 there were nearly 2,000 registered bingo clubs patronized by 3,000,000 citizens, three-quarters of them women. One company with eighty bingo halls made pre-tax profits of nearly three million pounds in 1971 and the estimated turnover of the whole industry is three hundred million. Betting shops number 15,500 and almost eighty per cent of the adult population bets on a classic horse race. Football pools cover an audience five times larger than that of bingo, and the major promoters operate Rolls Royces in order to bring the good news to winners in style.

With the adoption of private goals as public policy, public goals become in effect a kind of treason. Within peasant societies, where the largest unit of social organization is the family, the refusal of any individual to further the interests of the group except where they coincide with his own selfish interest acts as an automatic limitation on the social effect of all initiatives—since the efforts of one family to aggrandize are automatically resisted by a temporary coalition of their neighbors. The hope of material gain in the short run will be the sole motive for concern over public affairs in such a situation. The affluent countries of the West have now reached a position where the legal and economic framework within which their societies exist is determined by just such a coincidence of public and private interests as that operative in peasant societies. Where public interests do not coincide with private ones—as in the case of artificial restrictions on land value—recourse is made to a bureaucratic expedient. A social bureaucracy is invented and expanded to occupy the vacant space between the extinguished public interest and the private gratification of those occupying positions of exploitative advantage. Attempts to mobilize the dispossessed public interest—in the form of tenant associations, rent strikes, occupations and demonstrations—are characteristically denounced as though they were the work of other *private* interests, the consequence of a few *individual* "troublemakers" who have "stirred up" the people. This is because government today is characterized by a recognition only of private motivations, never of public. Hence the persistent denunciation of the popular defenders of the Catholic enclaves of Northern Ireland as "gunmen," "thugs" or "criminals." Hence also the characteristic defense against them which consisted in active attempts to facilitate their disintegration into smaller and smaller units.[29]

Such a refusal to recognize the existence of a legitimate public realm is at once the very foundation of environmental terrorism and also the clearest possible demonstration of its effectiveness. The abrupt disintegration of militant industrial action as soon as wage settlements are offered, the collapse of the working-class component of the May 1968 rising in France at a similar juncture, even the over-hasty burial of ideological differences between East and West as soon as trade agreements are signed—all indicate the impossibility of resuscitating an authentic public realm when the goals of the protagonists of all sides are dominated by private interests. The existence of a genuine public realm in any Western country is an accident of misrule which can almost always be patched up before any se-

---

[29] Press reports of the formation of "Women together," a nonexistent organization of Catholic wives opposed to violence, revealed this process very clearly. The London *Times* of April 4, 1972 reported the breaking up of a meeting organized by "Women together" by women loyal to the IRA in the Andersonstown district of Belfast. The alleged representatives of the Catholic public housing of the district in fact consisted of women from a nearby private housing estate.

rious disorders occur. The only price is the continued propagation of a believable dream of progress toward private wealth.

By and large the protesters who form the body of any popular social movement are willing, if not eager, to be bought off and absorbed into the realm of wealth and privacy that they assail. Their combination, their demonstrations, even their fervor exists only in pursuit of this end. Like prisoners in some surrealist drama where they exist outside the walls of the jail, the victims of environmental terrorism in the West can be forced to engage in meaningless work, persuaded to submit to palpably unjust distributions of wealth, tranquilized by the liberal distribution of chemical antidotes to despair,[30] *as long as the chance of private affluence remains, as long as the random, illogical pattern of admission to the citadel of comfortable privatization is not fully cut off forever.*

[30] Between 1961 and 1971 the annual number of prescriptions for psychotropic drugs increased from 32.2 to 47.8 million in Britain. Out of a total of 245.5 million prescriptions issued in 1970, 19 million were for sleeping pills of one kind or another, and 15.4 million for tranquilizers. Significantly, in view of their repressed position in society, 72 per cent of all sleeping drug prescriptions were made out for women.

CHAPTER FIVE

POLITICS: THE RAINBOW OF APPLAUSE

"You know something, Bebe?" President Nixon remarked to his best friend, Bebe Rebozo, one night recently. "I feel so alone most of the time. Right now, even though Pat is just in the next room and you are right here, I still feel alone. It's like feeling as though you were sitting on top of a bomb or something, and knowing it's about to explode. There's always the fear of making the wrong move, the wrong decision. How do I get away from this feeling?" But Charles Gregory Rebozo, the 55-year-old Florida real-estate tycoon who has become nationally recognized as Richard Nixon's closest friend, could offer only silent sympathy. "I just shrugged," said Bebe. "What else could I do?"

The National Enquirer, March 29, 1970

In the sense that prostitution was the guilty secret of the Victorian era, and success the secret of the age of affluence which is only now ending, so has privatization become the hidden theme of the present, the time of worsening. In the retrospective eye of history the spirit of an age can seem paradoxically to have been the very reverse of that which its leading citizens so confidently expounded in their lives. Like the two sides of a coin Victorian morality and Victorian exploitation war for mastery between the covers of books, as the faces of another, newer coin, social welfare and corporate greed, struggle for the mastery of the past quarter-century among the papers of the historians of the future. In each case there is an official preference and a free-lance denial, a conventional wisdom and an heretical hypothesis. In the past the heretical hypothesis has tended to become the conventional wisdom of the succeeding generation, hence our insights into the officially camouflaged infrastructure of Victorian life; but in the future we cannot be certain that this simple dialectic will continue to apply. Historically the conflict between rival explanations for the same events has seemed to proceed from the protection of certain interests on one hand, and the desire to expose them on the other.

In our own time this clarity of opposition has been confused by an unprecedented frenzy of inaction in the conduct of public life, a ruinous expenditure of energy with no issue in terms of great events or transformations. At the same time we have expressed a similarly unprecedented demand for the solution to a number of pressing social problems—unprecedented, that is, in the volume and amplitude of the voices raised rather than in terms of their real effect in bringing about change. Our era is distinguished by much public discussion of patriotism, security, prosperity, parenthood, social welfare, community values, law and order, to singularly little real effect. So much so that it is clear that all such talk is only camouflage to obscure a guilty but relished private indifference, a massive withdrawal from public life and from *de facto* responsibility for any of these matters.

Of all the arenas of public life, politics displays this paradox most keenly. At a time when development of the techniques of political management in the Western world appears to threaten the systematization of all democratic politics, calls for decentralization and community democracy flood the radical press and subsume the attention of students and activists everywhere. At a time when evidence of political chicanery, bribery, corruption and spying dominate media reporting of the American Presidential elections, the claims of politicians to be honest, principled and devoted to the public good know no bounds. At a time when the technical development of communications media enables opinion sampling, news reporting and campaigning to reach a higher proportion of the general public than ever before, public enthusiasm for politics, policies and politicians is remorselessly eroding away. In Britain for example the number of voters, relative to population increase and enlargement of the franchise, has barely held steady since 1945. In France a plebiscite held to determine the opinion of the people on the projected enlargement of the European Economic Community to include Britain, Ireland, Denmark and (at that time) Norway, was greeted with a massive 40 per cent abstention. And this despite the fact that President Pompidou had assured the electorate on television that the future of France, its people and their children would depend on their answer. In the United States the Presidential elections of 1968 saw Richard Nixon win with the smallest majority of the present century. His landslide victory four years later was achieved on the lowest poll (relative to the number of registered voters) recorded since 1948.

The disenchantment evidenced by these and similar indicators is of course not new. Public cynicism about politicians is as old as politics itself. The difference is that it has become sophisticated. The electorate of all Western countries is sceptical about the honesty and probity of its rulers—as indeed it has every right to be in view of the evidence of duplicity continually spewed out by newspapers, magazines, books, films and TV programs. The sophistication is to be found in the effect of this cynicism, which is apparently negligible. Whether the peoples of the West *believe* their governments or not seems to make very little difference to anything—as little in fact as the grinding repression which is traditionally supposed to be the lot of their counterparts in the socialist countries of Eastern Europe, the Caribbean and Asia. Just as the people of Soviet Russia, China and Cuba obstinately refuse to rise up and put their oppressors to the sword before making deals with the World Bank, so do the peoples of the West refuse to act upon the outrage of newspaper columnists and expel their corrupt and degenerate rulers. Despite the courageous activities of antiwar groups in the United States, the rhetoric of left-wing *comités d'action* in France and the dramatic exploits of urban guerrillas in West Germany, the vast majority of the population in all three countries plays willing accomplice to the crimes of power. The mob, once described as providence's device for meting out retribution to unjust governments, has retired from history because history has become largely irrelevant to its way of life.

This intractable state of affairs lies at the heart of the difficulties faced by those who wish to radically alter the system of government in the West. As the earlier quotation from Marcuse indicated, the enslaved masses do not wish to be emancipated unless emancipation means speedier access to the private satisfactions of affluence than the chances offered by the old, corrupt neocapitalist regimes that they know so well. Under a corrupt regime there is always the chance of private wealth, because that is the unspoken goal of all corruption. In contemplating a socialist utopia, a "happy land" such as the Republics of China or Cuba, there is the gnawing fear that *all* the loopholes will be closed, all the chances erased once and for all.[1] This fear underlies the political impact of affluence. The "apathy" so much criticized by Western political activists does indeed mask a guilty complicity with the *status quo,* and the reactionary stance of organized labor stems directly from it. In Britain the last decade of the former Amalgamated Engineering Union saw two elections for General Secretary decided on a total poll of 9 per cent of the membership, and one election for president decided on a poll of 6 per cent. In France the support which the CGT *(Confédération Générale du Travail)* gave to President de Gaulle during the events of May 1968 was purchased at the nonrevolutionary price of all-round wage increases—themselves swallowed up by inflation within months. As Jean-Pierre Vigier observed afterwards:[2]

Political and economic organizations founded to oppose capitalism have slowly acquired the same hierarchical structures and methods of acting as the system they claim to be attacking . . . Except for their rhetoric they have actively attempted to integrate their supporters into the system and have become incapable of proposing any meaningful alternative . . .

In other words they have become part of it. Like all shades of opinion represented in Western politics they have grown almost imperceptibly into component parts of the same thing. The acquisition and distribution of affluence has become their sole *raison d'être;* their apparent differences are but show. As

[1] The role of lotteries, prizes and gambling of all kinds in prolonging the patience of the underprivileged is well understood in political circles in the West. In Argentina media inflation of the story of a Paraguayan laborer's 330,000,000 pesos win on the football pools defused the political crisis of April 1972, in which the assassination by guerrillas of the local Fiat manager and an army general had brought the country to the brink of civil war. V. S. Naipaul, "The King over the Water," The London *Sunday Times,* August 6, 1972.
[2] Jean-Pierre Vigier, *The Action Committees. Reflections on the Revolution in France.* Ed. Charles Posner (Penguin Books, Harmondsworth, 1970).

a radical British printworkers' paper put it: "The affiliation of trades unionists to the Labour Party is like the affiliation of a condemned prisoner's neck to the hangman's noose." A clear perception perhaps, but under reigning conditions a totally ineffective one.

The idea of the affluent consumer life has become the most powerful weapon in the hands of any Western government. The consumer dream has an overwhelmingly incantatory effect. In Northern Ireland for example it makes sense of the Provisional IRA's bomb campaign to destroy the basis of employment in the province, for with the prospect of wealth finally extinguished the politicization of the whole population would be a foregone conclusion. But it also explains the countervailing efforts of the British government to pump in development capital and indeed their determined maintenance of public utilities and social-security payments in the former Catholic no-go areas, despite rent and rate strikes lasting over a year. It even explains the defeat of the Sinn Fein Irish nationalist party in the Irish Republic's Common Market referendum in May 1972, a defeat which in the long run probably sealed the fate of the IRA in the North. Seventy per cent of the electorate in the Irish Republic voted, 83 per cent of them in favor of entry into the enlarged European Economic Community with its improved employment prospects and higher prices for agricultural produce. Even in Dublin, where, a few months before, a crowd of 40,000 had applauded the burning of the British Embassy and called repeatedly for a united Ireland, the vote for prosperity overwhelmed the vote for tradition. The Sinn Fein party, opposing Common Market entry and invoking the ghosts of the martyrs of Ireland's bloody fight for independence, went down before the prospect of wall-to-wall carpeting and color TV.

To the radical political activists it must seem that the lustful accumulation of consumer goods represents the principal reason for the surprising longevity of capitalism, its projection forward into a kind of cancerous dotage with cells multiplying horrendously while cerebral control weakens by the hour. Once an activist begins to probe the pathology of this condition he runs the risk of exhausting his life in the process; it is not amenable to treatment for at the heart of political "apathy" lies the mainspring of consumer desire. Show me a family with two cars, Willie Loman might say, and I'll show you people who take no *real* notice of the dubious fiscal activities of their Supreme Court judges; who do not actively *care* about the progress or otherwise of the Vietnam war; who feel a mild surge of *pride* on learning that the former Prime Minister of France paid no income tax for five years; who dismiss as *carping* the news that the Anglo-French Concorde SST will not only cost ten times the amount estimated but be a commercial fiasco into the bargain. The affluent, the owners of their own houses, the followers of their own careers are unmoved (except to glee) by the tales of police brutality that fill the pages of the underground press and the "concerned" (but profitable) serious weeklies. They care not a fig for the independence of the judiciary, even less for the abrupt changes of allegiance that pass for foreign policy these days. Their interest in politicians is private, prurient and vengeful; they want scapegoats more than they want heroes.

Thus when a documentary film called *La Guerre d'Algérie* is shown to Paris cinema audiences ten years after the termination of the event, the appearance on the screen of Premier Guy Mollet explaining why army conscripts would have to serve thirty months instead of the normal draft period of eighteen, is greeted with cries of "Bastard!" while critics on newspapers recorded that the film made them "sick, sick to the stomach." Similar reactions had greeted an earlier documentary on the Nazi occupation of France and the extent of French collaboration. Public opinion, in its therapeutic indifference to the daily horrors of power wielded in its name, reacts with horror to events lived through but somehow ignored at the time. Similar reactions are no doubt already in store for the American directors of the Vietnam war once the dreamlike status of their present power is lost.

The vagaries of public opinion as revealed by polls are a clear indication that something more than indifference underlies such outbursts of displeasure or bitterness. Like a querulous old man who is really thinking about other things, public opinion contradicts itself ten times a day but still retains a cynical consistency. Why, if in May 1971 a Lou Harris poll showed that 69 per cent of the American people no longer believed anything the Nixon administration said about Vietnam, did a further poll, taken in May 1972, show that 76 per cent approved the President's action in mining Haiphong harbor? How, for a start, were they able to convince themselves that the harbor had been mined at all?

Anomalous results of this kind are not limited to the United States. In Britain a Harris poll on public attitudes to Common Market entry taken in April 1971 showed that while 62 per cent of the sample did not wish to go in, 82 per cent thought that Britain would go in anyway. A profound cynicism underlies such results, profound rather than superficial. The citizen does not care about "important issues" because he senses, rightly, that they are neither real nor important, nor can he influence them without throwing into jeopardy all that he has gained for the private enjoyment of his private life. He knows the difference between revolutionary politics that gets you in jail, and handshaking, tub-thumping, personal-calls-from-the-President politics that never changes a thing. The opinion-poll experts may have thought that they had found a "new, disgruntled voter" in the 1972 Presidential election, but in the end they were wrong. The 1972 voter shopped in the same old store because he preferred it, because he (correctly) identified it with the protection of his own cocoon of privacy.

The suburban U.S. voter (nearly 40 per cent of the electorate) chose brand X politics again, not because he was deceived by the unsubtle chicanery of the Committee for the Re-election of the President, but because he saw a threat to his standard of living in the end of American world supremacy, in the beginning of a more egalitarian social policy, in the admission of the arguments of draft dodgers, pot smokers and revolutionaries of all kinds if he voted the other way. He re-elected the President because he is less trouble than *Sieg Heil,* or Chairman Mao; especially because he is less agonizing than the confrontation with "real" issues promised by George McGovern.

"Real" public issues such as the war, corruption, crime, pollution, racial conflict, educational crisis, drug addiction and the revolt of the young are precisely the kinds of nightmare that the public wants its politicians to sweep under the carpet. Such matters cannot yet (or so far have not been) presented to the people in a form which makes it possible to consider them without panic. Until they are, any attempt to open the Pandora's box of "real" issues without at the same time promising to "stamp them out" poses a real threat to the public peace of mind because it must inevitably seem to place responsibility for confronting them onto *the community.* Because there *is* no community this responsibility is immediately interpreted as *blame* by every individual, blame for things that he hardly dares think about let alone accept responsibility for. The absence of an effective public realm in the Western world is nowhere more clearly seen than in the resistance its citizens put up to any kind of intelligent confrontation with these "real" issues. People prefer, literally, to pay private welfare organizations to tinker with the symptoms than to confront the disease themselves. Thus the McGovern campaign, larded with references to the crack of doom, and weighed down with *anxieties* over such "issues" as war guilt, amnesty and the corruptions of office, precipitated a Gadarene rush to escape the load of what was universally interpreted as *blame.* Thankfully the American people embraced their president's denunciation of this mon-

strous program. "McGovern," said Richard Nixon,[3] "is a man
who wants to add 82 million people to the welfare rolls and increase taxes by 50 per cent." That paltry "explanation" suf-
ficed because it was all that was needed. The result was a massive majority for the incumbent President who promised a new
era of peace, prosperity with reduced taxation, and a soothing
line with problems of the kind so artlessly publicized by his
nineteenth-century opponent. The Presidential election of 1972
was a triumph of private issues over public "issues." Even the
President's landslide victory was the achivement of a private
ambition, since few Republican candidates for the Senate or
the House of Representatives benefited from it. The triumph
of private issues explains why the President even gained from
the pattern of apathy which was expected to give McGovern a
fighting chance by causing a low poll. The Nixon slogan "Four
more years" conveyed a message to the electorate that most
commentators failed to grasp in their concentration on "the
issues" as propounded by his opponent. Nixon concentrated on
what he thought would be *the effect* on the public of concentration on the issues, and simply promised four more years of
freedom from the kind of anguish involved. Four more years of
relative affluence, relative security, relative evasion of the social
revolution that is implicit in any attempt to really come to
terms with crime, drugs, pollution and war guilt.

Was the electorate astute enough to understand this? That
is not the question. What is evident from the result is that the
corporate figure of Richard Nixon Limited was wise enough to
offer it to them. Gripped by Bismarck's old dictum that "The
mass of the people is inert," the vast majority of the columnists,
commentators and psephologists covering the election failed
to grasp the subtleties of that inertia, even though from the
very beginning of the campaign they had recorded abundant
evidence of it in innumerable significant anecdotes.

[3] James Reston, "Nixon Rides High on the Low Road," *International Herald
Tribune,* August 28, 1972.

A worker in a paper-processing plant in Ohio told a reporter during a visit by George McGovern, "I like what he stands for, I'm for Montgomery" (sic).[4] A woman in Milwaukee wearing a McGovern button called out "We love you" to Hubert Humphrey. "But you're wearing a McGovern button!" "Yes, but we love you, Hubert Humphrey."[5] Arthur Bremer, George Wallace's putative assassin, wrote during his wandering weeks as a political groupie, "Happiness is hearing George Wallace sing the national anthem, or having him arrested for a hit and run accident."[6] The majority of an opinion sample taken one week before the Presidential election, after two months of Democratic propaganda over the ITT scandal, the secret campaign fund and the original Watergate bugging incident, replied to the question "Has either candidate conducted a dirty and unscrupulous campaign?" with the answer "George McGovern."[7]

The perverse result of the opinion poll, the words of the "dull, but legally sane"[8] assassin, the Milwaukee woman and the Ohio paperworker are instructive. Although they might seem to emanate from the idiot fringe of political life they are also—if looked at closely—brilliantly satirical statements capable of raising canned laughter on the most sophisticated television show. To describe the soberly campaigning McGovern as "Montgomery," to wear a McGovern button and shout "We love you" to Hubert Humphrey, to fantasize about a racist chanting "Oh say can you see . . ." or explaining his way out of some Chappaquiddick-like catastrophe, to react to the loaded question of who is conducting a dirty and unscrupulous campaign with a deadpan "McGovern"—each of these is a bril-

---

[4] The London *Times,* April 29, 1972.

[5] *Time,* May 29, 1972.

[6] *Ibid.*

[7] *The New York Times* Yankelovitch survey, October 30, 1972.

[8] Description of Bremer offered by court-appointed doctor after his arrest on a concealed weapons charge on November 18, 1971, *Time,* May 29, 1972.

liant piece of dialogue, the product of sophisticated minds (both the perpetrators and the reporters), for all these jokes were publicized on a world scale. Bremer's observation alone is almost worthy of Lenny Bruce, and the reporter who dug it out from his papers after his arrest knew it. The poll result is like an exchange from Laurel and Hardy. Thus by a simple reinterpretation incidents which are normally passed off as the results of public apathy or stupidity can be seen as highlights from the *play* of an extremely sophisticated game between the public and its teams of corrupt and for the most part deluded politicians.

Politics in any consumer society is dominated by private interests, those of the voters as well as those of individual political teams. The "real" issues are merely part of the rhetoric of a game which requires a *pretense* that they are important as much as a covert acknowledgment that their importance is secondary in more senses than one. "The issues" are the first things to be forgotten in the aftermath of any major election; recent American and European examples clearly demonstrate this fact. In the 1956 Presidential election the major issues were a nuclear test ban and an end to the draft. In 1960 the burning question was the relative toughness of the two condidates over the shelling of the Chinese Nationalist offshore islands of Quemoy and Matsu. In 1964 the question was whether to end the Vietnam war or win it by the use of nuclear weapons. In 1968 the winning candidate declared that his predecessor's party had exhausted their opportunities to end the war without having done so. In 1972 the same candidate won again by promising "a new era of peace" even though he had been unable to end the war in four years. His opponent lost by concentrating on corruption in the incumbent administration. In Britain the Conservative party won the general election of 1970 because its leader promised to cut prices "at a stroke." There are a hundred other examples and in every case "the issues" are either forgotten or unresolved by the end of the victorious administration's term of office.

The ostensible issues of political life in the West are one thing, the real issues of private life and the pursuit of affluence are something else. We all know this, but as Charles Augustin Sainte-Beuve remarked of the prospect of our own deaths, we do not believe it. Successful politics in the latter part of the twentieth century results from the skillful selection of disguises for the private interests that any policy represents. The issues are merely a wardrobe—about as important to the success of a political program as are the costumes for the success of a play.

THE POLITICS OF SURVIVAL

However, it should not be thought that the crisis of political life in our time is solely a function of the preference of the public for private concerns. It has another facet of equal importance, which is the growing uninhabitability of the public realm under the pressure of media scrutiny, and the enormous price which individuals must pay simply in order to remain within it. The massive development of communications media since the birth of popular journalism in the latter part of the nineteenth century has had the effect of turning the world of politics into a transparent bowl within which everything can be seen and most things can be remembered. Despite steadily increasing expenditure on security and secrecy, up to and including the creation of private armies of spies and counterspies, developments in this field can barely keep pace with the technology of surveillance and the phsychology of the leak. Which is to say that even those who object most strongly to the demands of security and the advantages of espionage find themselves obliged to submit to the former and utilize the latter in the course of their political careers. Not only does the President of the United States feel obliged to travel in a 500,000-dollar armor-plated Lincoln limousine weighing five tons and equipped with a bulletproof plexiglass bubble which can be hydraulically raised when he wants to stand up and wave, but even Angela Davis is obliged to submit to the constraints of the bulletproof podium. Within hours of her acquittal on charges arising from the attempted escape of the Soledad brothers, she had received hundreds of anonymous death threats. Her nationwide tour to raise money to pay defense costs was dogged by white extremist picketing and elaborate security precautions. The fate of John Kennedy, Robert Kennedy, Martin Luther King, Malcolm X and George Wallace awaits every public figure who, perhaps through an imperviousness to experience, is able to convey weight and meaning enough to arouse the obsession of an assassin.

The incidence of political murder in the United States since 1963 has been sufficiently high to influence the political process on its own account. Not only present and past U.S. Presidents are guarded by secret service men, but also Vice-Presidents, leaders of the opposition and candidates for office. To the scrutiny of a jealous public looking on is added the blank reflecting stare of lenses and gun barrels looking out. The armor proliferates, the public appearances shrink, the distance between the people and their rulers increases. In the end only the Olympian unreality of television is left, and in politics, as in sport and entertainment, the Olympian view brings its own special brand of destruction. The depth and intensity of media scrutiny threatens the total being of the candidate for office in a manner which can be exploited by opponents who themselves remain anonymous. Consider the brief candidacy for the Democratic Presidential nomination of Senator Edmund Muskie from Maine.

Muskie ran as Vice-Presidential candidate with Hubert Humphrey in 1968 with considerable success. In the Congressional elections of 1970 he made an inspiring election-eve television address which effectively thwarted the Republican administration's attempts to link the Democratic party with rising crime, drugs and antiwar protest. By mid-1971 he was widely accepted as the Democratic party's best Presidential candidate for 1972, and nowhere more seriously than at Republican party headquarters. On the eve of the 1972 primaries a *Newsweek* state-by-state count showed him ahead in 29 of the 50 states; Muskie organizations were at work in 11 states and embryonic in 22 more. His full-time staff in Washington numbered over seventy, already busily soliciting the eight to twelve million dollars his campaign was expected to cost before the party convention in August. But odd portents had been observed. In July 1971 letters typed on facsimiles of Muskie stationery were sent to numerous Democratic Congressmen drawing their attention to a Lou Harris poll on the effect of the Chappaquiddick incident on Senator Edward Kennedy's popularity, an event which led to complaints about unethical campaigning. In February 1972, two weeks before the first primary contest in New Hampshire where Muskie was expected to trounce his competitors, a right-wing newspaper in the state, the Manchester *Union Leader,* printed a letter from a mythical "Paul Morrison," who claimed that the candidate had laughed at an assistant's sneering reference to Franco-American New Englanders (40 per cent of New Hampshire's registered Democrats) while touring a drug treatment center at Fort Lauderdale, Florida. Other "Canuck" letters later appeared but their source remained unknown until September 25, 1972 when a Washington *Post* reporter claimed that one of President Nixon's 522 "special campaign advisers" had confessed to having written at least one of them. Hot on the heels of the first "Canuck" letter came a Manchester *Union Leader* reprint of a trifling story which had already appeared in *Newsweek* and *Women's Wear Daily* to the effect that the candidate's wife smoked a lot, had once asked reporters if they knew any dirty jokes and in any case enjoyed pre-dinner cocktails. Worse still, as the New Hampshire vote approached Manchester residents began to be awakened at early hours of the morning by telephone calls purporting to come from the "Harlem for Muskie Committee" urging them to vote for the candidate because he had been "so good for the black man." Plagued by headlines such as "Moscow Muskie," "Flip-flop Muskie," his organization racked with inexplicable disappearances from files, floods of fake handbills, forged letters and damaging leaks of confidential information, the Senator finally rounded on William Loeb, editor of the Manchester *Union Leader*. Standing on the back of a truck parked in front of the newspaper's offices, in the middle of a snowstorm in full view of numerous reporters and CBS television cameras, he began to berate the archconservative Loeb—a man who always carries a gun to "protect himself from criminals." Quoting from a *Union Leader* story about his wife headlined "Big Daddy's Jane," Muskie speedily lost his composure and began to weep. "This man doesn't walk, he crawls," he sobbed. The news flashed around the country, around the world. The following day Loeb editorialized that "Losing control of yourself and weeping is not something that you do if you are a real man." *Time* magazine quoted an unidentified member of the Democratic National Committee who drew comparisons between the President forging new alliances in China and his putative successor blubbering on the back of a truck. Senator Henry Jackson, a fellow Democrat contender for the nomination, was reported to have wondered how the candidate would face up to Brezhnev. Muskie himself tried to recover like an old trouper and a few days later was joking about the incident in Boston. "When my wife packs for me nowadays she puts in six extra handkerchiefs."

Muskie's showing in the New Hampshire primary, though not disastrous, was dismal. During the week between New Hampshire and Florida his campaigning for the latter poll was marred by the distribution of further fake handbills listing the alleged matrimonial indiscretions of Senator Hubert Humphrey and Senator Henry Jackson and drawing conclusions favorable to Muskie. On March 14 in Florida the candidate came in third behind George Wallace and Hubert Humphrey. On April 4, in Wisconsin, he captured only 10 per cent of the vote and ran fourth behind George McGovern, George Wallace, and Hubert Humphrey. On April 17 a Muskie fund-raising dinner at the Washington Hilton was disturbed by the unsolicited arrival of three hundred dollars' worth of liquor, 200 pizzas, cakes from the Watergate pastry shop, a dozen African diplomats and two magicians—one specially flown in from the Virgin Islands. On April 25, in Pennsylvania, the candidate again ran fourth behind Humphrey, McGovern and George Wallace. Shortly after, his organization demoralized and bankrupt through the defection of donors dismayed by his performance, Senator Edmund Muskie withdrew from the primary contest.[9]

A more celebrated and disastrous case concerned Senator Thomas Eagleton of Missouri, who was briefly George McGovern's running mate until it was "discovered" that he had undergone psychiatric treatment earlier in his career. For reasons which are not immediately clear in retrospect this admission, in addition to unsubstantiated charges of drunken driving, caused his removal from the Vice-Presidential nomination even though public-opinion polls indicated that a majority felt he should retain the post. As if this were not enough, well-substantiated allegations were later made that the psychiatric treatment issue as well as the groundless charges of drunken driving had already been used against Eagleton during the campaign in which he gained his Senate seat in 1968 and were

[9] This brief summary of Senator Muskie's campaign for the Presidential nomination was assembled from reports in: *Newsweek,* January 10, 1972; the *Guardian,* March 2, 1972; the London *Times,* April 22, 1972; *Time,* March 6 and 13, April 3, 10 and 17 and May 29, 1972; *International Herald Tribune,* October 12, 14 and 15, 1972.

not in fact the closely guarded secret that his detractors maintained.[10]

Robust assertions that incidents such as these merely demonstrate the "weakness" of the politicians concerned and their inability to withstand the stresses of public life, in fact pose more questions than they answer. The mode of survival in political life today is in many ways even more alarming than its destructive power. Today's successful politician learns that he can only "live" his public life if he accepts the dissonance between it and any private reality he may once have known. When John Lindsay can have tawny medium peach rubbed over his face and extra eyelashes painted in without a qualm, when Richard Nixon can accept Charles of the Ritz Sand Liquicreme and appealing green contact lenses while reading the scripts of television commercials for himself; when any politician can see and accept the loss of himself in favor of the mobile support and playback system that he becomes—then he has learned to survive. But in what form? What is the conglomerate of a team of script writers, a make-up artist, a plastic surgeon, a team of doctors, some armed guards, miles of audio and video tape, a market-research team, several advertising agencies, private planes, armored cars, squads of security men,

[10] ". . . The undersigned was involved in the Humphrey effort from May to November 1968 and spent a considerable time in Missouri. At that time Tom Eagleton was campaigning for the U.S. Senate. His medical history was well known throughout the state and even the false rumors of arrests for drunken driving were widespread. These items were well known not only to me, but to many other participants in the Humphrey effort as well as to key people within the Democratic National Committee. Many of these people came to hold responsible positions in the McGovern campaign. In view of these circumstances Senator Eagleton had every right to assume that Senator McGovern had knowledge of both the medical history and the false rumors when he chose the vice-presidential nominee. Senator Eagleton also had the right to assume that the matter was a dead political issue. He won a hard-fought primary against two formidable opponents, the incumbent Senator . . . and ex-Ambassador Davis who reportedly leaked the arrest rumors . . ." Extract from a letter by T. A. Nikoloric published in the *International Herald Tribune*, August 8, 1972.

a bulletproof podium and a clutch of rich corporate backers? As Joe McGinniss revealed in a celebrated study of political merchandising[11] such a corporate entity is almost infinitely malleable within the constraints of the interests he represents. His subjectivity to all intents and purposes surrenders to the objectivity of his own projected image.

The paradox of the era of press and television scrutiny, where the role of the politician is to defend the private interests of the consumer, is that he sacrifices not only his own privacy but also his personality. Only the remolded individual can survive the pressures of political life; only the rebuilt ego can undergo the chemical change from human being to "personality" that public life requires. The survivors in political life, like the survivors of the world of entertainment and the world of sport, are individuals who have grasped the idea of *another reality*. Their fate is to live in it forever, because to them it becomes more real than any other world. In assuming the burden of allowing himself to be presented as living in a world of weighty decisions, agonizing choices and honors wisely bestowed, in permitting the charade of the book-lined study, the healthy outdoor life, the church credentials, the obedient wife and children, the successful politician becomes the victim not merely of the private consumer's interests but of his *dreams*. The media that remorselessly stalk him, equally remorselessly escalate the demands that the people make upon him. He is condemned to the spiraling pursuit of continuous orbit, away from reality altogether, off into THE ISSUES to drag from them something that looks like *the substance* of the impossible dreams of his supporters. Thus when Hubert Humphrey, exhausted by a quarter-century of campaigning, greets his followers in Wisconsin with the words, "I am thinking of three elections today. I am thinking of Wisconsin on April 4th, the

---

[11] Joe McGinniss, *The Selling of the President* (Trident Press, New York, 1969).

general election on November 7th, and *that final election in the sky when we all meet our heavenly destiny,"* he is begging. Begging for one last trip into the wild blue yonder before they take his license away.

Inevitably, linked as they are by a common experience of the epic void of leadership which lies at the end of the rainbow of applause, politicians of all parties are more similar than they are different. Accommodations with political opponents exceed demonstrations of antipathy in all the democracies of the West. In Britain the leader of the loyal opposition will personally award an honorary Doctorate of Technology to the Prime Minister of a government whose policies he has described as the most reactionary of the present century. In the United States a leading Democratic politician will be appointed Secretary of the Treasury in a Republican administration and will later head an organization of party turncoats prepared to vote for their opponents' Presidential candidate. In West Germany opposition parties will abstain from a major vote on the signature of a peace treaty to conclude the long overdue business of the Second World War, so as to permit the treaty to be signed without actually espousing it themselves. These accommodations very rarely break down: physical violence between politicians did occur in the House of Commons in 1971, on the occasion of a free vote on Common Market entry, and in the following year an Irish member of parliament briefly assaulted the Home Secretary over his apparent indifference to the killing of thirteen civilians during an army operation in Ulster, but such events are exceptional, like the fights occasionally observed in the United States between the campaign workers of opposing candidates, or indeed the bloody Democratic convention of 1968. By and large a passionless truce reigns at the heart of the democratic system and it is a truce which will grow year by year more confirmed. The party is no longer important, the issues are no longer important, the rhetoric is no longer important. All that matters is whether the politician is "sane" or "mad," whether he flies in the same TV-fed, high-consumption nirvana as his constituents —or whether he somehow still thinks people can be persuaded to give up their cars, color television sets, freezers, credit cards, stereo systems and multiple video phone extensions.

In his Faustian deal with what we shall define in a later chapter as secondary reality, the late twentieth-century politician has submitted himself to technique, to never losing his place and never forgetting his lines. With the development of communications technology this technique has been extended into the systematization of the political machine itself, which has thus become an integral part of the vast consumer servicing system. Today a computerized network can saturate an electoral area with "personal" telephone calls from candidates whose market-research teams have already determined the "area of concern" of selected individuals. A tape-recorded message from the candidate can be played over the voter's telephone explaining just what the candidate would do about that particular "problem" if elected; in addition the voter can be put in touch with a local "expert" who is also a supporter of the candidate. All this by remote control using a computer center hundreds of miles away, some tape cassettes, a little local market research and the purchased services of the telephone company.

"Technique" in this sense was admirably defined by Jacques Ellul twenty years ago as "the totality of means rationally arrived at and having absolute efficiency (at a given stage of development) in every field of human activity."[12] The process applies equally to politics, entertainment, defense, sport and athletics, education, medicine, motoring, planning and design, even housework and the organization of daily life. Technique is triumphant in the modern world; like technology, it delivers the goods. It works where tradition, superstition, faith and

[12] Jacques Ellul, *The Technological Society* (Paris, 1954).

magic fail: it reduces unpredictable events to a very low rate of occurrence—perhaps eventually it will reduce them to zero. In achieving this result, however, it cannot evade the implications of the law of entropy: in exhausting magic—which is the inexplicable, unpredictable but also irreversible *event*— it also exhausts interest and enthusiasm except in determined opposition to itself. The consequence of the triumph of technique is the annihilation of involvement *within* the process, which thereafter becomes configurational instead of active. Politics in the private future will assume the character of show business, sponsored show business, prerecorded show business, the show business of the advertising agency rather than the circus. The lessons of technique cannot long be lost on political participants, for they are already clear to the public. Few vignettes in the 1972 Presidential election were more pitiful than the sight of future shocked McGovern ringmasters Frank Mankiewicz and Pierre Salinger protesting that the polling stations were not yet closed and the votes not yet counted when a television interviewer, equipped with an accurate NBC computerized prediction assured them that the game was up on the basis of a four per cent sample.

Confusion and ambiguity are as essential to vital politics as they are to workable taxation. Without loopholes and concessions, taxation systems would be inoperable. Without confusion and ambiguity, politics must collapse amid elaborate jeers. The optimization of political technique in the service of the private consumer has reduced confusion and ambiguity in politics to almost zero, with the result that the art of the possible is ceasing to be.

There is no way to reinvest political life with an authenticity outside its service to the private realm because its public inauthenticity is to a great extent structural. As we have seen, the very formation and organization of the urban areas of the consumer world, the mobility of the population, the universality of consumer service needs, all have conspired to rob political representation of any basis save its direct economic concern to the individual. Thus issues which fall outside the scope of the narrow world of the pleasures of consumption cannot influence an electorate which is determined above all things to protect those pleasures against a sea of "issues" which are merely tricks to take them away. *Unless the global crises of twentieth-century life can be presented within the narrow context of the job, the house, the car and the holiday, they will not even be recognized by the voter. Thus action on these matters must inevitably take place outside the political system, and the political system itself be drawn into the defense of private interests against such measures as are taken. Politics in the West has become a secondary reality; its dissonance with felt reality is universally understood but kept secret. The future of politics lies in the extension of this unreal world into a final combat with the intractable realities of the public past.*

CHAPTER SIX

SPORT:
FROM REPLAY
TO RIOT

At 15:45 hours on September 5, 1972, the twentieth modern Olympic games held in Munich, West Germany, came to a temporary halt. At 04:30 that morning two members of the Israeli team had been shot and since then a further nine had been sitting on beds, bound hand and foot, in one of the apartments allocated to them in the Olympic village. While boxing, basketball, fencing, football, handball, volleyball and equestrian events took place around them, their captors, eight members of the Black September Palestine terrorist organization, negotiated unsuccessfully for the release of 200 fellow guerrillas in Israeli prisons. By midnight that night all of the Israeli hostages, five of the terrorists and a German policeman were dead after an abortive West German attempt at rescue. The following morning a memorial service took place in the Olympic stadium with 80,000 people present: during the afternoon of the same day the games resumed. British team captain

Lynn Davies was reported to have commented on the tragedy of the preceding 24 hours: "It makes long jumping seem somehow less important. But of course you have to keep going because the Olympic ideal is worth preserving."[1] The London *Daily Mirror,* the newspaper with the biggest daily sale in Britain, announced that it was the task of the "international community" to root out terrorism.

The tragic events of the twentieth Olympiad, like the shooting of 200 demonstrating students which preceded the nineteenth Olympiad in Mexico City, were dramatic indications of the impending collapse of the world of sport in the late twentieth century. Like the world of politics, the world of sport has shown itself to be as much a victim of the breakdown of *community* as any other manifestation of public life. Not that this collapse is dependent on the activities of Palestine guerrillas, or even on the increasing politicization of the games themselves. It is not. Nor is it solely the result of exasperation and despair over arbitrary disqualifications, dope tests, psychological disturbances or octogenarian incompetence at the helm. Sport is doomed because it is in the grip of the same process of exploitation as that which in the case of industry says that if you are not growing, you are shrinking. This exploitation, this technologically reinforced giantism, will not be arrested until all popular enthusiasm for sport has been exterminated by the prior extermination of the principle of free competition itself.

If, as we have seen, the combination of media scrutiny and public affluence has had the effect of reducing politics to the status of a rigged game with violent overtones, then similar forces in the shape of media scrutiny and government and commercial sponsorship have had an analogous effect upon sport. Just as the destiny of consumer politics is indifference

[1] Frank McGhee, "Munich: Gold, Silver, Bronze and Lead," *Daily Mirror,* September 10, 1972.

laced with violence, so is the destiny of shamateur and professional sport an uneasy mixture of the same ingredients. Violence has become as inseparable from sport in the television age as sport from lavish sponsorship by governments, corporations and spectators. Nor does the analogy between politics and sport end here, for once again efforts to eradicate violence tend to exacerbate apathy and *vice versa*.

Sponsorship in sport as in business means investment, and investment is under most circumstances attended by risk. In sport, as in business, the heavier the investment the greater efforts are made to reduce the risk involved by those who stand to lose. From the point of view of the competitor in any sport, sponsorship automatically reduces the risk he or she runs in their specialization, but the sponsor himself also wishes to reduce the risk to his own investment and his efforts to do this can threaten the competitive nature of the event itself. Sponsorship, as later examples will show, tends automatically towards an equalization of performance and minimization of the risk of unplanned mishaps which together endanger the competitive principle. Inevitably a closely fought contest of any kind where the outcome hinges upon split microseconds or disputed readings of the regulations is inherently unsatisfactory for competitor and spectator alike, not least because it throws into sharp relief the irreducible imperfections of the game itself, whether it be table tennis, soccer, motor racing or athletics. The final irreducible risk—which is the enthusiasm of the competitor and the spectator—thus assumes an importance which increases in proportion to the closeness of the contest. For example the massive investment, worldwide competition and unprecedented television audience marshaled together for the Munich Olympics of 1972 demonstrated the knife edge which separates global enthusiasm from anger and disgust simply because of the number of dead heats, split or unpopular decisions and barely justifiable disqualifications which marred so many events. During the games, even before the intervention of Arab terrorists, more commentators spoke freely of the end of the Olympics and the collapse of international athletics than ever before.

The vast concatenation of chauvinism, expenditure, training, skill and preparation had simply succeeded in pushing the games themselves to the limit of their feasibility as competitive events. Absolute dead heats in swimming, unseemly disputes over basketball scores, dubious drug disqualifications, incompetent refereeing at boxing, unbelievable changes of official ruling over the legality of pole vaulters' poles—a thousand and one absurd details combined with the major political disqualifications to dominate news reporting of the games. As a result the games became unplayable, the athletes could no longer win with certainty nor lose with grace: the spectators no longer argued about performance (which had become the one certain commodity) but concentrated on medical and legalistic matters. The games have toppled from their great eminence into the shadow of complete abandonment because the technology of media scrutiny and the massive insurance that accompanies heavy investment have pushed performance beyond the point of competition. In ancient Greece the athletes competed against each other and no one recorded times: today all athletes compete against the clock, and the clock has beaten all of them.

The fate of massively subsidized international athletics as witnessed by the Munich Olympiad in full view of a hundred million television viewers is only the most spectacular of the crises attending sport in the era of media scrutiny. The growth of sponsorship has all but extinguished amateur status in games as diverse as ice hockey and chess. The sponsored or professional player may be assured of prosperity for the length of his contract period, but the position he has taken has had an irreversible effect on the games themselves. Fixtures have become such weighty matters of investment that squabbles between trainers, managers and officials elevate every infringement and dispute into a major political row with the enthusiasm of the players and the allegiance of the spectators perpetually in the balance. Player behavior dominates reporting of tennis; crowd disturbances haunt soccer, American football, ice hockey, rugby, almost any sport capable of generating press or television coverage. Sports commentators occasionally put two and two together in an indictment of a particular game, but the consequences for sport as a whole are seldom dwelled on—perhaps they are unthinkable for those whose livelihoods are bound up with them.

For the purpose of an analysis of this process of decline we can ignore the heavily publicized questions of cortisone-induced performance in athletics, disqualification in skiing and golf, racial disputes in cricket and tennis, and the high incidence of non-fixtures in boxing. Not because they are irrelevant, but because the process of collapse to which they attest can be better explained by considering two popular but very different sports in more detail. Soccer and motor racing are beset with analogous problems, and problems created by attempts to deal with those problems. Let us consider them in turn.

SOCCER: THE LIMITS TO GROWTH

Soccer, as it is played today, is a game of largely British origin. Its social background is ambiguous since although it is considered a working-class game both Oxford University and the Old Etonians have won the annual Football Association cup. The real growth of the game dates from the late nineteenth century when the Football League was founded in opposition to the relatively aristocratic FA, with a rapidly growing number of affiliated clubs from the industrial towns of the north of England. In 1889 the Football League had 12 clubs; by 1921 the figure had grown to 86. Since then the number has slightly increased but at least fifty of the present clubs have existed for years on locally organized lotteries, sweepstakes, donations from supporters' clubs and by mortgaging their own soccer grounds. In 1971–72 seventy-six clubs ran at a loss and eleven just about broke even; the remaining few made a profit. At the time of its maximum growth soccer was an underfinanced working-class sport played on grounds that were not equipped with grandstands or any spectator facilities. Nonetheless it throve on Depression conditions; like Roller Derby in the United States it benefited from unemployment, poverty and the absence of competitive attractions. During the 1930's, crowds of nearly 40,000 often watched reserve teams play one another.

Like live theater and vaudeville it largely collapsed under the impact of television during the 1950's but by that time it had been exported to most of the nations of the world, including Eastern Europe and Latin America. In Britain, triumph in the 1966 World Cup led to a resurgence of popular enthusiasm for the game with greatly increased gate money for important fixtures and massively increased television coverage. Extensive programs of grandstand building and other ground improvements followed. In 1961 the uniform maximum wage paid to all professional players was abolished and the earnings of the most successful footballers began a rapid rise that has not yet ceased. Today, bonuses of £5,000 and more are paid as an inducement to victory in a single match. At the same time the process of buying and selling promising players burst through all financial restraint so that transactions involving up to half a million pounds have taken place in recent years. This system not only had the effect of increasing the value of good players to the clubs that owned or coveted them, but also began to create conflicts between the demands of club and national fixtures.

In the last ten years the players themselves have attained a celebrity status unknown to their predecessors, and with it external interests in the form of associations with sportswear manufacturers, retailers and various branches of the entertainment industry. The footballer as celebrity has become a male model, a film star, even a pop singer. During the winter of 1971–72 twenty songs were recorded by soccer teams, some of them rising high in the charts. The season itself has recently been extended to take advantage of increased popular enthusiasm and to maximize the earning power of the game.

Under such pressures the players, catapulted in their teens into wealth, fame and an unprecedented level of exploitation, inevitably react like politicians and other Saturnalian heroes. Some reify their personalities, become simply the creatures of agenda and external demand; others crumble, retreat, or become the victims of their own appetites and opportunities. As early as 1965 charges of betting and corruption in First Division matches led to three famous players serving jail terms and being banned from the game. George Best, a leading star, fled the country in the spring of 1972, claiming that the stresses of his life had reduced him to the level of consuming a bottle of whisky a day and spending sleepless nights. His much-publicized withdrawal from the game led characteristically to a lawsuit between the newspaper chain to which he was contracted and the rival paper to which he gave a resignation exclusive. Another England player whose wife was expecting a baby abandoned the game in order to make his newly purchased house fit to live in by the time of her confinement. Such evidence of stress at the center had long since been matched by rising security problems at the fixtures themselves; the mass of working-class supporters who had sustained the game for so long became an embarrassment to its upward social mobility and recently acquired status as a debating ground for intellectuals. Soccer hooliganism joined drunken driving and drug addiction on the media index of social decline. Violence between rival players as well as rival gangs of supporters began to dominate the image of the game. Slowly its intrinsic imperfections began to emerge as a kind of cancer which only drastic surgery in the form of "tough disciplinary measures" could hope to contain.

In January 1971 at Ibrox Park, Glasgow, unruliness among a crowd of 50,000 led to a panic in which sixty-six people were killed. An official inquiry held closely packed standing spectators to be the cause and recommended a reduction in the permissible number of unseated spectators. Alterations to the stands at major clubs to conform to this recommendation were expected to cost at least £50,000 a year in lost gate money alone. At the same time it was suggested that adequate crowd control should be made a condition of club licensing, itself unknown until the 1971–72 season.

Now it might seem that a combination of adequate ground security, middle-class attendance and yet more television coverage could still assure the game a future of sorts, even if far removed from the category of low-cost spectator entertainment. Unfortunately, consideration of the effects of covered grandstand construction *and* increased television coverage seems to indicate that the cancer cannot be defeated so easily. Just as stand construction shifts the social level of the spectators as well as removing them from close physical proximity to the game, so does it change their perception of it—an effect which is to be observed tenfold in the case of television coverage. Far from losing his sense of the general progress of play, the grandstand or TV spectator actually gains from his Olympian detachment. The final exclusion of teenage soccer gangs from football grounds in the pursuit of safety and good behavior might seem to be the answer to the difficulties of the game, but in practice it seems likely that it will exacerbate spectator and player dissatisfaction for the following reasons.

Soccer is a game played on a flat pitch by opposing teams of eleven men. Foul moves and infringements of the regulations are controlled by a referee and his assistant linesmen. Because of this topography the referee is obliged to monitor play by running about the pitch to keep within sight of the ball. This process is imperfect, as can be readily grasped from the description; incidents often take place when the referee is unsighted and because there is no replay capability, disputes over position and movement can only be settled by the referee's ruling. This unsatisfactory but hitherto unavoidable process has been thrown into sharp relief by the development of television coverage using zoom lenses and slow-motion replay capability together with the more obvious advantage of a viewing position high above the ground. Television monitoring of the progress of play—sometimes shared by as many as twenty million viewers (only about 600,000 buy in at the turnstiles every week)—has become infinitely more precise and reliable than any referee's partial perspective. To some extent the grandstand viewer too shares this advantage.

At the same time the stratification of clubs into more or less equally matched divisions, together with the mercenary purchase of the best players, has made the performance of competing teams more equal than was the case in the past. Consequently the most important matches are also the most closely fought, with a corresponding emphasis on referee decisions, both in the matter of foul moves and in disputes over position. The conflict inherent in this situation finally exploded during the 1972–73 season when a First Division player, who had appealed to the High Court over a fine and suspension awarded him by the Football Association Disciplinary Committee after an incident two years before, won his case chiefly as a result of his presentation of a television recording of the match in question, which refuted the charges of the referee who had made the original complaint. Within days of this judgment several daily newspapers began reproducing stills from the television films of important matches showing contentious incidents. Further appeals were immediately announced.

Quite apart from the nightmarish prospect of suspended

decisions, and players watching the cameras instead of the referee when in any case they should be watching the ball, such incidents represent only part of the malaise which equal performance and media scrutiny have brought to the game. In Continental football the penalty kick (a shot at the opponent's goal awarded for some infringement of the rules by a member of his team) has become the standard means of scoring goals in top-line matches. During the 1971–72 season Moscow Dynamo beat Dynamo East Berlin 5–2 on penalties alone. Where no infringements occur—or when none are detected—the result is often a goalless draw. During the same season Celtic and Inter Milan played for a total of three and a half hours without scoring. In Berlin the return match between West Germany and England during the quarter-finals of the European Nations Cup also ended in a goalless draw but with fouls predominating in the second half to such an extent that spectators began to leave the ground in large numbers long before the end of the game.

Internal matches display the same tendencies. The FA Cup Final of 1972 was won by Leeds over Arsenal by one goal to nil; there were twenty-four fouls in the first thirty-six minutes and five players were reprimanded by the referee. Forty-eight hours later Leeds played another game in the Football League Cup, losing by two goals to one. Their chance to equalize was lost through the referee being unsighted during a foul by an opposing player: television viewers saw the foul replayed, grandstand spectators only saw it once but rioted in protest with the result that eighty people were injured. A few weeks later on the European circuit Glasgow Rangers beat Moscow Dynamo before a crowd of 110,000 in the Camp Nou stadium in Barcelona: the Rangers supporters rioted and police charged them. Over a hundred were injured and the same number were arrested as street fighting and hotel wrecking continued into the night. The Russian team demanded a replay and appealed to the European Football Union's disciplinary committee. A

London newspaper columnist commented that "By perpetuating the obsolete values of aggression, 'winning' and irrational group loyalty, football as a national institution tends to corrupt and deprave."[2] The growth of media coverage of player and spectator violence may encourage such a view, but what will be the consequences for the game if it comes to predominate? Under a system introduced for the 1972–73 season, twelve reprimands by a referee will lead to automatic player disqualification. In the first five days of the season 125 players were reprimanded and eight sent off the field. All announced their intention of appealing, and that was *before* the High Court decision based on television evidence.

The more closely the game is perceived the less satisfactory it seems to be. Consequently all efforts to remove or pacify the spectator by giving him an Olympian view of the struggle only stimulate him more. The inadequacies of the referee system are impossible to rectify without either removing him from the field to watch through monitor screens (and thus sacrificing real time in the contest itself) or stripping him of his powers altogether. Efforts to predict the outcome of games by computer have already been tried; pressed further, they show every likelihood of converting the dangerous and evocative physical struggle into a kind of electronic simulation, like the celebrated electronic attempt to rob Muhammad Ali of his heavyweight boxing title. Tendencies in this direction can already be observed in the grafting onto lotteries and random number competitions of the imagery and semiology of real games. Pinball games called "Grand Prix," "Big Game Hunt" and so on, racing car simulators, water ski simulators, even the game circuits which will soon be optional extras for television sets—all hint at the emasculated future of real games when their practical viability is ended by over-exploitation. Computerized voting for media politicians is already foreseen.

[2] Richard Neville, London *Evening Standard*, May 11, 1972.

Why not electronic substitutes for the complexities and contradictions of the soccer field? These are matters to which we will return in a more general context, but for the present it is sufficient to conclude that the logic of their development seems inescapable through the exhaustion of their "real" forerunners.

In the case of soccer, the more spectators the richer the game. The richer the game the more equal the performance of competing teams. The more equal their performance the more emphasis on referee decisions. The more emphasis on arbitration the more incitement to violence or dissatisfaction on the part of player and spectator alike. The more violence and dissatisfaction the greater the reliance on "discipline" and TV coverage. The more "discipline" and TV coverage the more arbitrary will seem the rule of the referee and so on. The game will descend into a miasma of modified rules, deferred decisions and eventual spectator apathy. All these tendencies are already evident in microcosm; ground attendances in 1972–73 were down ten per cent on the previous year and several spectacular improvement schemes were halted as a result. The scissors effect of heavy investment and equalized performance has cut the game to ribbons. What remains is a top-heavy structure of such precarious value that the *simulation* of competition must soon supersede its reality. As in the case of politics there is no way back to authenticity because the corruption is structural, the entropic price of success as a spectator sport. The computer, the pinball machine, the electronic replay, the surrogate contest—yes. The game—no.[3]

---

[3] The growing popularity of Roller Derby in the United States confirms this evolution. After a lapse in popularity during the 1950's and early 1960's, this simple roller-skate battle is again in the ascendant with a record attendance of over 50,000 at Chicago White Sox Park in September 1972. Denied sporting status (like wrestling) by serious sportsmen, the game combines minimum complexity with maximum violence and immaterial scoring—thus evading the difficulties that are described above.

GRAND PRIX, THE ONE-WAY FANTASY EXPRESS

The terrible fate of the Olympic Games,[4] and the doom that hangs over the future of professional soccer have their analogues in the contemporary crises of *Grand Prix* motor racing, a very different but similarly afflicted sport. There "technique" refined by heavy sponsorship is erasing the necessary imperfections of the motor race at such a rate as to make collapse inevitable before long. The same near-equality of performance can be observed as in top-class soccer and the proliferation of regulations is already developed to a much higher degree. Sponsorship, creating problems similar to those experienced in athletics, and attempts to reinforce competitor and spectator security have been developed to such extremes that the complete exclusion of the spectator in favor of a television audience can be foreseen and indeed is popular in certain categories of motor racing already.

Although motor racing antedated popular motoring by some decades, the fantasy association between sports and high-performance saloon cars and the racing circuit has for many years acted as a hidden subsidy for the sport itself. In the past many motor manufacturers maintained racing teams at great expense and the practice is by no means extinct despite the recent withdrawal of Ferrari from the circuit, the last of the major motor manufacturers to do so. Mercedes, Alfa Romeo, Aston Martin, and many others ran racing teams, some until comparatively recently. Today Ford alone among the major corporations develops racing engines, the remainder having withdrawn from *Grand Prix* competition altogether. To be sure, many small manufacturers compose cars around components made by others and many sports car manufacturers race their cars, but the day of the major manufacturer sponsoring

---

[4] The reported refusal of the city of Denver, Colorado, to stage the 1976 Winter Olympic Games may reflect the beginning of a resistance to even the most commercially profitable manifestations of international sport.

his own racing team is over. A powerful reason for this change, apart from the growing expense of international motor racing and the largely surrealistic relationship between today's *Grand Prix* car and its road-going equivalent, has been the change the years of affluence have wrought in the status of popular motoring. From being a pastime, driving has become a way of life involving almost all the able-bodied persons in any consumer society. Today's automatic, air-conditioned, stereo-equipped passenger car, its driver strapped in and blood tested against the influence of alcohol, navigates solid streams of traffic under the remote control of symbols and colored lights. There is no "winning," no "fastest time of the day," no checkered flag in popular motoring—unless it be in daring defiance of a code of regulations which yearly grows more comprehensive. Hence the increasing interest of motor manufacturers in rallying, autocross, stock-car racing and other hybrid sports which do at least use cars recognizably derived from road-going models. Racing cars pure and simple are out on a limb; their closest cousins, open sports cars, are already dying off at the hands of the insurance companies.

With these peripheral factors in mind the present terminal growth of *Grand Prix* racing under the sponsorship of tobacco companies, airlines, cosmetic manufacturers and so on is easier to understand. The process of "winning" has been as effectively hijacked by product manufacturers as has the quality "charisma" been quantified by political managers. The derailing of the fantasy express running from road to circuit has left the heroes up for grabs, and the consequence has been the sponsored racing team.

Sponsorship by other than motor manufacturers began before the Second World War in Fascist Italy, where, as in Nazi Germany, the government itself financed development for reasons of national prestige. With the development of consumer societies this source of revenue died out and instead a heterogeneous collection of mass-consumption product and service suppliers took over the role. The present state of the art can best be assessed by recounting the tale of the "John Player Special." In 1971 an agreement was reached between the Imperial Tobacco Corporation and Lotus cars to the effect that in 1972 the Lotus Formula One *Grand Prix* car would race under the name of a branded Imperial Tobacco cigarette called "John Player Special." The cars duly appeared in the same color and style as the cigarette pack of the same name: the word Lotus appeared nowhere, not on the car, not on the fixture lists, not in the publicized results. Only the name of the tire supplier and the oil company providing the fuel marred the image of a racing advertisement for lung cancer without a government health warning. Despite problems over television coverage, where cigarette advertising is banned, the venture proceeded successfully until the British *Grand Prix* of April 1972, which, sponsored by Imperial Tobacco, was tentatively renamed "John Player *Grand Prix*." Patriotic drivers and enthusiasts protested[5] at the renaming but to little effect. The real difficulty arose because Marlboro, a rival cigarette manufacturer and car sponsor, refused to allow its own BRM cars to carry stickers advertising a rival brand of cigarette even though this had, ingeniously, been made a condition of entry. Marlboro was of course capable of tying up other international *Grands Prix* so that "John Player Specials" would be obliged to undergo the same humiliation elsewhere. In the event Imperial Tobacco abandoned their *Grand Prix* title.

Problems of this kind might seem to be destined to expire with the suppression of cigarette advertising itself, which is probably only a matter of time, but the same kind of conflict plagues sponsorship from other sources as well. Oil companies,

---

[5] "The word 'British' does not seem to have the same meaning as when our fathers fought for their country and a land fit for heroes to come back to-- if they survived . . . This is a disgusting insult to all those who still put Britain first." Extract from a letter by driver John Surtees published in *Autosport,* January 13, 1972.

for example, sponsor both cars and race meetings, consequently occasions arise where a competing car bearing the
name of the oil company which fuels it is obliged, according to
the rules governing entry into the event, to carry an advertisement for the rival oil company sponsoring the race—thus
arousing doubts as to which miracle ingredient does in fact
contribute to its (hopefully) astounding performance. During
1972, European racing teams reacted differently to this conflict. Castrol-sponsored cars carried Duckham's, Shell and BP
stickers, while "John Player Specials" raced without Shell
stickers in defiance of regulations. This situation remains unresolved at the time of writing, but even an amicable solution
will simply shift the squabbles of sponsors to other more
crucial areas. All the limitations on freedom of use which
plague the popular motorist have analogues in the world of
Grand Prix racing: the proliferation of regulations alone has
called forth a whole new bureaucracy in recent years and
behind this too lurks the unseen hand of the sponsor, striving
to reduce the risk that is inseparable from the very idea of
competition.

Paid officials called "scrutineers" now examine cars before
and after races to ensure that they comply with exacting regulations governing power and weight. Like the disputed referee
decisions which can turn a soccer match into a kind of court-
room drama exasperating to player and spectator alike, so can
scrutineers' judgments threaten the very principles of motor
racing. At a Formula Three race held at Brands Hatch, a
famous British circuit, on March 16, 1972, scrutineers spent
four hours examining the cars after the finish. They found that
the first *five* cars past the checkered flag had in fact been
ineligible for the race, principally through being underweight.
The first eligible car (which had finished sixth) had been
driven by a man whose own record of offenses under the same
formula had cost him £1,000 in prize money. His reward for
scrupulous honesty on this occasion was to witness the disqualification of the winner and the fining of the next four

drivers £20 each. This figure, subtracted from the then winners' £200 purse, of course amounted to a positive inducement to infringement. The matter did not end there. The disqualified driver then challenged the accuracy of the weighbridge and in consequence even the revised results were declared provisional pending the arrival of a government inspector whose visit could not be arranged for several days.[6] Now this sort of outcome to a race is not unusual, nor is it limited to single-seater cars; major rallies, which are at present heavily sponsored by motor manufacturers, have a history of similar scandals. Whether they indicate the impracticability of the regulations themselves, the obstructionism of the scrutineers, or the inveterate dishonesty of competitors is of no importance. Such results damage the reputation of the sport and flood competitor and spectator alike with dismay. A week's perusal of newspaper or TV reporting of all sporting events will yield a hundred similar examples from skiing, riding, athletics and golf. Scrutiny exposes the imperfection of any competitive enterprise; those imperfections are what makes competition possible; when regulations finally extinguish inequalities competition becomes impossible.

As we have seen in the case of soccer, the problem of crowd security and its treatment are tending in equal measure towards the extinction of the game. In motor racing too circuit safety is claiming its victims, and the first casualties are the spectators themselves. During 1972 GPDA[7] and CSI[8] regulations required considerable alterations to a number of *Grand Prix* circuits, which had the effect of removing all spectators from close proximity to moving cars. At Oulton Park in Britain these "improvements" involved the construction of seven-foot-high banks of earth reinforced with paving stones and railway sleepers which, combined with Armco steel barriers and wire screens, had the effect of reducing the spectacle of racing cars

---

[6] This account is taken from *Autosport*, March 23, 1972.

[7] *Grand Prix* Drivers' Association.

[8] *Commission Sportive Internationale*.

to a distant view of helmeted heads moving at high speed. At an estimated cost of £50,000 these works greatly reduced the number of spectators the circuit could accommodate, and in consequence admission prices were raised. Safety alterations of this kind are not limited to established circuits whose original design might be considered unsafe at the speeds reached by cars today. Entirely new circuits such as Nivelles in Belgium and Estoril in Portugal demonstrate the same ruthless segregation of cars and spectators. The provision of broad runways either side of the track effectively limits spectator participation to expensive grandstands built above the pits. Before considering the prospects for spectator-free televised motor racing we should perhaps examine in more detail the background to regulations which on the face of it would seem to be destructive of the very sport they aim to protect.

The GPDA and the CSI are both driver organizations and all demands for improved circuit safety emanate from them. This convention, however, merely masks economic realities because attempts to limit the danger inherent in almost all competitive sports proceed not from the cowardice of the competitors but from their *value* to the sponsor or manufacturer where one is involved. Danger to spectators is only a serious matter if a record of accidents begins to discourage people from visiting the venue—and there is no evidence of that happening to motor racing, even at Le Mans, where spectacular crashes involving large numbers of spectators have occurred. At Indianapolis crashes offer the chief means of differentiating the performance of otherwise identical cars, but because spectators are seldom involved little effort is made to contain them. Consequently it is true to say that attention to circuit safety in *Grand Prix* racing, which has apparently become an obsession in recent years, has in fact merely kept pace with the wildly escalating cost of the sport and the correspondingly increased value of the machinery, skill and advertising revenue tied up with it.

As if to demonstrate their indifference to safety regulations imposed by their own representative bodies, two GPDA drivers —Pedro Rodriguez and Jo Siffert—appeared driving sports cars on the Francorchamps circuit during 1971 in spite of the fact that the GPDA and the CSI had banned it for Formula One racing some time before.[9] Both were later killed on circuits thought to be safe. Once again the real obstacles to safety are the conditions of the game itself. Of course drivers do not want to get themselves killed, but they do want to race in fast cars; and if that were not exciting and dangerous nobody would do it, let alone watch it. The dangers of motor racing not only attract the spectators who constitute its value as an advertising medium, but also underwrite the fantasies and projections on which modern rapid-obsolescence, automobile sales are partly based. Safety regulations governing the design of cars and circuits as well as the conduct of race meetings and rallies may well be able to reduce the element of danger in motor sport to zero, but in doing so they will confirm the separation which has already occurred between that sport and popular motoring. Safe motor racing is like dangerous driving, a non-starter. So what is left for the sport? In all probability nothing for *Grand Prix* racing except a rapid decline; for hybrid forms of race which use variants of production cars in order to retain some sort of manufacturers' sponsorship there remains the possibility, already explored with rallycross, of televised meetings held with no spectators present. This type of motor sport involves little or no expenditure on the circuit, no expensive security arrangements, a high-performance differential, and close identification between competitive and production cars. Nonetheless even at this embryonic stage its simultaneous pursuit of manufacturer sponsorship and dependence upon television coverage threatens escalation into the world of the politics of investment. Like

[9] *Autosport,* March 16, 1972.

stock-car racing in the United States, televised rallycross leads directly to extensive car modification, a proliferation of regulations designed to limit it, and thus in turn to disqualifications and disputes—all intensifying with the equalization of performance that sponsorship brings. The ultimate destination of such "growth" was exemplified by the organization of the 1972 Le Mans twenty-four-hour race for sports cars. Although no privately entered car has won this race for twenty years it is still regarded as the basis for a whole year's advertising by the winning manufacturer. At different times, Jaguar, Ferrari, Ford and Porsche have dominated with expensive works-entered prototypes. In 1972 the French organizers changed the formula for the engines of cars running in the most powerful class so as to exclude the previously triumphant Ferraris and Porsches, then, with the race started and finished by the President of France, the first French victory since 1952 occurred. Matra cars, built by a subsidiary of France's leading manufacturer of missiles and weapon systems, took first and second places. The victory—like the Mercedes and Auto Union *Grand Prix* victories of 1934–39—assumed a political significance, and derived from political chicanery, utterly unrelated to motor sport.

The combination of media scrutiny and sponsorship means quite simply the extermination of real competition in all professional spectator sports. One by one they will follow the same path of ruthless exploitation, economic giantism and functional collapse. *Grand Prix* motor racing, like politics and soccer, will find no way back to innocence—only a projection forward into a willfully sustained illusion, a secondary reality.[10] In the

[10] Instructively, emphasis on outside sponsorship has given *Grand Prix* racing teams a new responsibility—to make cars and drivers available for display purposes at exhibitions, stores etc., where the sponsor wishes to promote his wares. Since the expensive cars are not easily made available during the racing season one sponsor, Marlboro cigarettes, commissioned six fiberglass replicas of their current Formula One car for the purpose.

meantime, just as such elementary conflicts as Roller Derby
threaten to succeed to the popularity of the old classic games
of footwork and agility, so in the world of automobile racing
the spectacle of demolition derby and the motorcycle jump
looms large on the horizon, the specter of the *"auto"-da-fé* of
the future. In California a demolition derby involving only
post-1970 cars (among them a Cadillac Eldorado and a
Lincoln Continental Mark IV) was held in 1973 with such
celebrated American track stars as Bobby Unser, Parnelli
Jones and Roger Ward driving. The event ended with many of
the 23,000 spectators invading the arena to loot usable parts
from the wrecks.

The sport of single-handed ocean racing, itself barely ten
years old as a sponsored activity, has already run through the
stages which in the case of soccer and motor racing took the
best part of a century. From a half-crown bet between two
British yachtsmen over an Atlantic race in 1960—sponsored
by the London *Observer*—it has escalated until by 1972 it had
become an international contest between professionals backed
by world-wide companies. The boats themselves are now
specially designed and built, single-handed craft costing up to
£120,000 each and useless for any other kind of sailing. Efforts
by organizers to control technical development and sponsorship are evidently failing with the introduction of electrically
operated self-steering equipment and brand-named boats—
both in defiance of regulations. In the latter case characteristic
ingenuity is to be observed in the use of names such as "Peter
Stuyvesant," commemorating the founder of New York City
of course, but later abridged to "PS" after strong objections; and
"Strongbow," allegedly named after the second Earl of Here-
ford (who died in 1176), and not the cider of the same name
marketed by the boat's sponsors.

In all such cases near-equal performance becomes the one
certain commodity: sponsorship and the interpretation of increasingly complex regulations the real ground on which the

prize of "winning" is won or lost. Professional boxing offers a clear indication of the disintegration to which all competitive sports can look forward. World heavyweight championship bouts are dogged by political disqualifications, battles between promoters, lawyers, accountants and officials. The leading contenders themselves have already achieved each-way status with almost equal amounts of prize money and percentages going to winner and loser; there is already a powerful lobby in favor of banning the sport altogether on humanitarian grounds. It is in any case reduced to heavyweight contests as far as the majority of the public are concerned. Who even knows the name of the world middleweight champion, unless he was once Edith Piaf's lover?

By one of the ineffable ironies of history the Church of England passed through the process of sponsorship *en route* to decline. Livings for clergymen fell into private and institutional hands as a result of struggles between rival factions in the nineteenth century and many religious trusts were established in order to ensure the succession of "right-thinking" incumbents. Even today half the 10,000 livings available in England are in the hands of private patrons including individuals, institutions (such as Smiths Crisps and Sun Allied Insurance) and the Crown. Unfortunately the irreducible risk, public allegiance to the spectacle, collapsed in the interval and the private award of livings is now regarded as an embarrassment rather than an exercise of power.

CHAPTER SEVEN

THE COMING OF SECONDARY REALITY

The time has come to consider in more detail the internal mechanism of the process of media scrutiny outlined in the preceding chapters, and to attempt to define the term "Secondary Reality" which has been used to describe some aspects of its influence. The phrase itself is a neologism meaning the conscious erection of a preferred reality over that which demonstrably exists, but the complexities of its operation in the modern world necessitate some preamble, since its emergence as a means of escape from an intolerable primary reality considerably antedated its present development into a highly sophisticated technique.

Secondary reality as a means of survival emerged from the industrial urbanism of the nineteenth century. Then, as now, it represented a means of reversing the growing administrative insignificance of the individual by finding new meanings in the anonymity of city life. Its roots as a creative phenomenon can be traced back to the French Symbolist poets who for the first time drew the minutiae of everyday life—tavern signs, fairy stories, the Latin of the mass and phrases from old songs—into a system of imagery which was later to receive intellectual underpinnings from psychoanalysis and visualization from Dadaism and Surrealism. During the course of the twentieth century these combined insights fused into the commercial arts of advertising and entertainment and thus progressed as received ideas into the culture of mass consumption. This process, aided as it was by the rapid technical development of communications and entertainment media, coincided with the decentralization of urban life itself, so that the physical and psychological foundations of suburban living can be said to have evolved simultaneously.

Paralleling this conversion of the wildest fantasies of poets and the most extreme images of the artistic *avant-garde* into the stuff of popular advertising and entertainment, has come a revolutionary disturbance in the balance of the mass media themselves, culminating in the absolute domination of television. Although books, magazines, newspapers, radio and cinema coexist with television, one by one they seem destined to succumb to its (or its technical derivative's) remorseless competition. Radio is now a showcase for the record industry; the cinema, despite cunning twists and turns into multiscreen, miniscreen, social realism, romantic fantasy and bloodletting therapy, still contracts, surviving largely as a result of a technical and creative overlap with television itself. Newspapers have reached a crucial stage in the cycle of sponsor-induced growth described earlier. In Britain in 1955 eighty-eight per cent of the population read a morning paper and the remaining twelve per cent could not read; that was one year after the introduction of commercial television. By 1965 readership seemed set into an irreversible decline with advertising revenue (paying for up to sixty per cent of the production cost of a quality paper) shifting steadily to television. Five years later, with papers selling over a million copies closing down or merging with rivals, Fleet Street, despite half a century of printing news on the back of advertisements, had mushroomed to the point where one million pounds profit required a turnover of two hundred millions. Today printing unions and press barons alike freely issue predictions of collapse.

Television, on the other hand, forges ahead. New channels are opened, color processes refined, video cassette and game attachments planned: after a quarter of a century of growth, during which the number of television sets in England alone increased from 2,000 to 15,000,000 and one-third of all cinemas closed down, the medium retains a potential as great as that of the cinema at the dawn of the talkies. The technical and commercial development of television cannot be halted, only its independence is in any danger, and that independence, the querulous criticism of the *status quo* mounted by a handful of producers and commentators, can be easily crushed as events in France after the 1968 uprising clearly showed. In any case, just as advertising revenue is more important to any newspaper or magazine than the political or social opinions it expresses, so are other things far more important to television than the emotional or political bias of its programs. Like live theater it thrives on lost tempers and unplanned incidents, but these can just as easily arise in connection with flower arrangement as with radical social criticism. The important thing is the retention of the audience, and to this end time itself is contracted into an endless present. Every film becomes so interspersed with fliers for its successor, every drama so larded with the essence of the next night's or the next week's equivalent, that judgment is perpetually suspended, orientation permanently lost. In talk shows and newscasts this phenomenon of continuity presents the performer with a reason for future entrances, for a last word, then a final last word, then (in response to changing circumstances) further last words so that challenge becomes impossible in real time. The only thing you can do is turn it off—which is like stopping a game of tennis by running away with the ball.

In political terms this is important because it partially explains the power of television as well as the curious *indirectness* of its effect. Television politics reduces the right of spontaneous dissent to the equivalent of a self-applied blindfold and gag. Poor performances or ill-considered words can be erased from consciousness overnight; in every way the medium seems to be the perfect vehicle for mass necromancy, and yet even those who claim to use its techniques for limited and specific ends seem unable to get exactly what they want from it.

The doubt is important and not an afterthought because with television, as with the automobile, the private house, the newspaper, the advertisement, all the shibboleths of Western living, there is more at work and at stake than the manipulative power of politicians and big business. What they rule also rules them in the sense that they must continue to supply what the majority demand, even if that is only more of the same. In deferring its final judgment for commercial reasons, television, more than any other medium of communication, suspends judgment. The apparent struggle between monsters with great power and humane men with great influence is somehow transmuted into something more acceptable by television, something *endless*. Because the medium cannot afford to deliver a final judgment—it signally failed when it tried to do so in the case of Richard Nixon, whose political career was at one time thought to have been ruined by his lamentable 1960 showing against John Kennedy—its political influence consists largely in its ability to *distract* rather than to analyze. Television perpetually suspends judgment because it exudes a continuousness which is in itself more significant and influential than any message it may attempt to convey at the same time. There is a Spanish expression, "He is only telling the time," which is used to deride those who continually talk but never reach conclusions. Television continually tells the time, as surely as if it were a speaking clock. If there is a documentary it is "The Tuesday Documentary"; if there is a play it is "The Wednesday Play"; if there is a news bulletin it is "The News at Ten." Every Tuesday there will be a documentary, every Wednesday there will be a play, at ten o'clock every night there will be some news. Even as you watch you are promised that there will be more, same time, same channel, tomorrow or next week.

This "telling the time" is, of course, a characteristic of newspapers that appear every morning or evening or weekend, magazines that appear every week, and books that appear every month. There are also fashions that appear every spring and new cars every year. These things are normal, they are part of a pattern of life. And that is exactly the point. Television is part of a pattern of life, a large part of it, part of a reality in which the promise of the program schedule is as important as the information any program conveys. But television is no ordinary part of normality because it also *makes things normal,* things as outlandish as a documentary about mental illness, a commercial for detergent, a political harangue, an earthquake, a war, a scandal or a walk on the moon. The television receiver is a magical object like the car, the washing machine and the freezer; but *much more magical* because it packages and homogenizes fragmentary aspects of reality. It constructs an acceptable reality out of largely unacceptable ingredients. No individual exposed to the physical reality of half a dozen of the events depicted on the news at ten could slump into an armchair half unconscious with boredom afterwards. No one person could have survived a bridge collapse, emerged from a ten-year jail sentence for spying, campaigned with the President, fought unseen guerrillas in Oman, covered the trial of a well-known politician accused of drunken driving, interviewed the defendant in a successful libel action and described the car crash which blinded him in one eye.

Television, queen of the consumer durables, is also the

principal assassin of public life and community politics. It absorbs the deceptions and evasions of the real world, mixes them with its own inherent deceptions, and thereby creates a new reality of its own, a reality more acceptable by far because of its *modulation* than the fragmentary glimpses of the real thing that occasionally prompt outraged citizens to write to the newspapers. The crisis of television begins when you stop watching it. Until then it exudes *secondary reality,* the synthetic social glue of consumer society.

In order to explain what secondary reality is and how television actually creates it we must begin with an historical example. In a short book entitled *Why don't we learn from history?* the military historian B. H. Liddell Hart recounts an anecdote from the First World War in which an eminent French general arrives at a certain army corps headquarters at a critical moment in the German breakthrough of March 1918. He issues orders giving the line on which the troops must stand that night and from which they must launch their counterattack in the morning. After reading these orders the corps commander exclaims: "But that line is behind the German front! We lost it yesterday." The French general, with a knowing smile, replies: "That is for history to decide."[1]

Now, the infamous conduct of the general is a perfect example of the workings of secondary reality. He confronts the experiential wisdom of the corps commander with a challenge—you prove that what you *know* is true really happened. I say that my version is true because it is beyond your power to disprove it. Even if it were not, you still would not do it because you gain as I do from a general belief in my version. As a result of this exchange, secondary reality in the form of the inspiring defense of an overrun position enters the history of the war.

---

[1] B. H. Liddell Hart, *Why Don't We Learn from History?* (Allen & Unwin, London, 1944).

Take another and quite different example. The art of fishing —as opposed to the industry of fishing, which uses simple physical traps—consists in convincing the fish that the baited hook is not a trap but food. For centuries this was done by actually dangling morsels of food before the fish in its normal feeding ground, but there is another way, which is to simulate the action and vibrations of the small fish upon which the hunted fish normally preys. This is usually done by towing a special device or lure through the water in such a way as to deceive the fish into thinking it is its natural prey. The perceptive mechanism of the fish, like all perceptive mechanisms, can only discriminate within well-defined limits. Like a human being looking at the flashing images of a cinema screen and thinking that he sees movement, the fish looks and listens to the lure and thinks that it recognizes food. This advertisement explains the process perfectly:

The Vibro's secret of taking fish is the pulsating vibration of the unique blade design. Even at the slowest possible rate of retrieve the Vibro spins, giving off the sonic vibrations that drive fish to a feeding frenzy.

The Vibro Sea Spoon is, for all practical purposes, a small fish, even though it is made of stainless steel and plated brass. It does not look like a fish to any human being, but then a photograph of a man does not look like a human being to any animal. There is a process of deception at work in both these examples which exploits the limits of the perceptive or reactive system which operates in any given set of circumstances. It is the mechanism of secondary reality.

In philosophical as well as optical terms television is founded on deception, just as film is founded upon illusion. Moving pictures do not move, they flash like bullets from a machine gun onto the screen in rapid succession, and the illusion of movement they create is founded upon the phenomenon of visual persistence, which itself results from the delay between the registration of the image by the retina and its recognition by the brain. The gap is tiny, about one twenty-fourth of a second, but it makes a whole world of illusory movement possible. Although television images are constructed by a different process of linear scanning the same phenomenon works there with the difference that the image is electronically reflected rather than recorded, which means that unless it is deliberately recorded it is lost as soon as transmission ends. These minor differences apart, the two media share a capacity to create an illusion of reality which has philosophical implications extending far beyond their technological capabilities.

Television and the cinema can so engross a viewer that for long periods of time he can be said to be the inhabitant of a kind of halfway world, somewhere between tangible reality and total hallucination. This phenomenon is not, of course, the invention of electronic media, for it has a genealogy immeasurably longer than that of the cinema. Religious ritual, theatrical performance, drug-induced trances and visions, history contains evidence of the existence of culturally significant, secondary-reality states as far back as records of human behavior extend. Heaven, Hell, Nirvana, the Dream Time, all represent psycho-technically constructed states of consciousness with central roles in the value systems of the societies to which they belonged. The major difference between these historic prototypes for secondary reality and their twentieth-century counterpart lies in the unprecedented technical performance of television and the cinema, and their saturation distribution throughout society. Secondary reality in the Western world has become universally accessible, something it could never become in any economy of scarcity. The composite psycho-technical products of consumer society limn the landscape of our secondary reality in the same way as the mystical objects of more primitive societies defined the secondary reality that they knew. Only the scale of the operation is different, and because of its remarkable information-carrying capability the television set has become the most magical object of all. Its value, and its cost in terms of energy and investment consumed, are thus difficult to exaggerate. Its magically tranquilizing effect, to the extent that it can blur the distinction between primary and secondary reality on an enormous scale, makes it powerful medicine indeed.

The Western world has, to be sure, divested its dream machine of the religious and mystical trappings that were integral with secondary reality in previous centuries. Its very technological facticity would seem to exclude mysteries of this kind. And yet the dreams and images of consumer life, the *value* appended to quasi-useless utensils such as rapid-obsolescence cars and cosmetics, suggests symbolic rather than concrete worth. A television commercial, for example, is part of our social environment, a psycho-technical product of the optimization of technique described earlier, and yet also a complete world from which messages reach us—as Orson Welles once said—via the lens of the camera and the magic of the cutting room. It is the *completeness* of this world, faltering and poorly defined as it is, that gives the television image its extraordinary power to confuse one reality with another. To all intents and purposes the subtitled word "simulation" is the only difference between an animated television reconstruction of a spacecraft docking exercise and satellite-relayed television pictures of the real thing. What, then, would constitute the difference between a fake news film of the President of the United States of America signing a peace treaty in Hanoi (subtitled "simulation"), and a TV newscast of the real thing taking place? The question is important, but before it can be answered a further attempt to elucidate the nature of secondary reality as presented by television must be made.[2]

---

[2] Concerned about this problem themselves, as a result of the successful impersonation of leading politicians by satirical comedians, the BBC issued a code of practice for producers in 1972 stipulating that all impersonations must be clearly indicated and subtitled if necessary.

First, we must accept that a fundamental deception underlies the whole process of television transmission unless it is
continuous, live and takes place in real time. Any televised encounter between politicians which is edited or reassembled
from prerecorded ingredients embodies this deception—as does
any mimed performance by a singer, any news bulletin, or any
commercial. The disparate assembly of images appears as a
single continuous form. This of course is true in a way of most
printed information, but the high information content of movement—which alone compensates for the comparatively poor
definition of moving as opposed to still pictures—elevates
television to an altogether different order of magnitude. A TV
commercial represents a deception precisely because of the
success with which it portrays a series of apparently unrelated
images as a single process with a single meaning.

Consider an ancient example which can be interpreted in
an unusually topical sense. The Greek philosopher Zeno used
the flight of an arrow as a paradox to illustrate the impossibility of movement. To say that an arrow released from a bow
moved in a line through the air was, he said, to claim that it
could be in two places at once, because at any single instant
it could be shown to be stationary and the multiple of a number of stationary positions was not the same as movement.
There could be no question of movement except as an illusion.
The truth of course is that movement is indivisible and to break
it down into an infinity of static positions is simply to *simulate*
movement, not to re-create it. This simulation, as used in
animated cartoons, works with the human eye because of the
fact of visual persistence, but in doing so it involves embarka-
tion on a voyage of deception for the viewer who now "sees"
because of the *inertia* of his optical system rather than through
its performance. Thus when we perceive movement on the
screen, and when we accept the product of editing as a smooth,
linear process, we react exactly as the fish reacts when he
"sees" food in the shape of a steel spoon.

In visual terms this means that apparent life, or reality, can be given to simulations (which is all the flickering images of a cartoon or a strip of movie film really are), quite apart from the events or processes they seek to portray. We accept as real something which is no more like reality than a steel fish lure is like a fish. The re-creation of the flight of an arrow by means of animated drawing is only a simulation of what is perceived of the arrow's flight—but it serves well enough to communicate the idea. In the same way a television commercial which can establish a domestic scene in a couple of seconds by means of sounds and reflections in kettles, windows and taps, somehow entraps a reality in that process which is "good enough" to convince the viewer: a reality, in fact, which is as necessary to the success of the commercial as the bow is to the arrow that it shoots.

The measure of secondary reality is the life it gives to what is in origin merely a simulation. What is seen is important, not what happens—and what is seen is not even what is shown. Thus secondary reality, the reality of media, is a psycho-technical construct: a meaning which comes into existence as a result of the combination of technical approximations with optical shortcomings. The television commercial—in proportion to its length often the most expensive type of film made anywhere—is a perfect module of secondary reality. What it does, with fifteen seconds of edited film, is to convert the factitious primary reality product it advertises into a passport to another world. By presenting the product in association with social situations in which it can help you win, the commercial converts the process of buying it into a public confirmation of the private entry already made into the garden of secondary reality. Consumer society is a form of barter for dreams; the product is something you buy in order to be worthy of the dream that goes with it. *The commercial is legitimized by the product,* not the other way around. Hence the meaninglessness of consumer products in the world of primary reality (who needs a vaginal deodorant?), and their *charismatic power* in the secondary-reality world entered via TV. The extent to which such products as automobiles, detergents, cosmetics and other fripperies are actively sought in the world of primary reality is really no more than an indication of the extent to which the seeker wishes to live permanently in the dream world with which they are associated. Thus the irony of the automobile purchased as the legitimization of the dream of a flying arrow—a means of escape from the crowded, polluted world of primary reality—which turns out to be an object capable only of an infinite series of static positions, literally as well as figuratively. If one could buy a car and drive it on the endlessly open road of a simulator, then the triumph of secondary reality would be complete. But that, though possible, is expensive and technically difficult—and in that expense and difficulty is to be found the chief weakness of secondary reality in a world whose energy resources may be inadequate to complete the social transformation from actuality to dream. Secondary reality, like space travel, offers a means of escape from the intractable contradictions of primary-reality life. But, as in the case of space travel, the penalty is the enormous energy requirement of remaining in orbit instead of remorselessly sinking back into the old, polluted atmosphere.

This paradox grasped, it can be clearly seen that the fate of the politician and sportsman in the modern world—like that of the consumer product—is to be marketed in the dream world of secondary reality but employed in the obstructive, factitious world of primary reality. Disappointment is inevitable. No personality promoted to power and influence by the dream machine of TV can ever live up to the irrational hopes invested in him by the consumer: the most he can reasonably expect is to be able to deploy sufficient energy to remain in orbit, and keep his supporters in orbit with him, for longer than his predecessors.

This situation is the product of the tangle of secondary-reality promise and primary-reality performance that constitutes public life today. Because the new industrial state cannot deploy sufficient energy to lift the consciousness of every one of its subjects into continuous secondary-reality orbit, the *events* of public life still take place on the ground. The absolute dissatisfaction which underlies both the rapid rate of obsolescence of "personalities," and increasing popular disabusal with public life, finds its origins here. Security through video-taped politics may well safeguard the lives of performers better in future, but unless techniques are rapidly developed for promoting secondary reality on a continuous and massive scale, public disorder, violence and apathy will continue to increase—or so it will appear to those in power. At present the real performance of any politician, entertainer or sportsman must dismay those who somehow expect a physical analogue to the therapeutic mime which takes place nightly on the screen. This is inevitable. The expectations themselves are almost comic, as Philip Slater has explained in *The Pursuit of Loneliness*:[3]

We still wait optimistically for some magic telegram informing us that the tangled skein of misery and self-deception into which we have woven ourselves has vanished in the night. Each month popular magazines regale their readers with such telegrams: announcing that our transportation crisis will be solved by a bigger plane or a wider road, mental illness with a pill, poverty with a law, slums with a bulldozer, urban conflict with a gas, racism with a goodwill gesture . . . Whatever realism we may display in technical areas, our approach to social issues inevitably falls back on cinematic tradition, in which social problems are resolved by gesture . . . a series of climactic movie scenes in which a long column of once surly natives, marching in solemn silence and as one man, framed by the setting sun, turn in their weapons to the white chief who has done them a good turn, or menace the white adventurer's enemy (who turns pale at the sight), or rebuild the missionaries' church, destroyed by fire.

[3] Philip Slater, *The Pursuit of Loneliness* (Allen Lane, London, 1971).

Such endings, alas, belong only in the world of secondary reality. In practice, the outcome is more likely to resemble My Lai, Kent State, or Bloody Sunday in Londonderry. The contrast between "tough measures" as conceived and outlined in a political broadcast, and the real *effect* of such measures is absolute—and so is public rejection of the reality of their failure. The massive public outcry in favor of Lieutenant Calley, convicted by a military court of killing over twenty unarmed civilians, reflects not so much the lurking savagery of the average American suburbanite as his refusal to be dragged out of the theater and into the world. If Errol Flynn can capture Burma, Robert Taylor fight from his own grave in Bataan, Robert Mitchum save Mai Britt's drunken husband from the Chinese army in Korea, and John Wayne make South Vietnam safe for hero-worshiping slants; then surely court-martialing Rusty Calley is like . . . like . . . drawing an enormous sexual organ on Rupert Bear! For which despicable act the editors of a British underground newspaper were sent to jail[4] in 1971. The efforts of U.S. personnel to save the crews of aircraft shot down over North Vietnam—which in one celebrated case cost thirteen lives in order to save one—often fall into a category inexplicable in any other way than as efforts to emulate the secondary-reality heroics of a generation of war movies.

In cases like Kent State or Bloody Sunday, courts of inquiry are not simply whitewash jobs, although that is what they inevitably appear to be. They are dramatic and expensive attempts to reconcile the two realities—to provide a rationalization for events which in retrospect seem to have promised disaster with a certainty unclear only to the protagonists them-

---

[4] The three editors of the London underground magazine *Oz* were briefly jailed in 1971 for attempting to "corrupt and deprave" the public by distributing a "Schoolkids' issue" dealing with children's lib, but featuring a hitherto virginal strip-cartoon character, Rupert Bear, armed with an enormous penis in the act of raping another innocuous character from the same strip, Gypsy Grannie.

selves. Abuse and rock-throwing on one side and half-trained men with guns on the other might seem to guarantee bloodshed, but when it comes the participants as well as the viewers are surprised and the proceedings of the court of inquiry reflect their disbelief. This is because the original circumstances of the outrage are as enmeshed in fantasy and posturing as the outcome is finalized in blood. Seen in reverse, the whole phenomenon is unintelligible because it only ever made sense as the random product of an official threat made as a result of a forgotten incident, counter-threats uttered later, and finally the half-accidental clash of the luckless participants.

In the event, these collisions between primary and secondary reality are relatively rare, like air crashes, and the publicity that surrounds them is really a testimonial to the unremarked completion of a thousand uneventful flights. We *assume* that we are going to travel safely and we *know* that it is better to do that than to arrive. If we keep the in-flight stereo headphones jammed into our ears maybe we won't even hear the plane breaking up. Certainly we will not hear the noisy contradictions of public life—the sound of the President of the United States describing himself as a "deeply committed pacifist" in a year when his administration spent 64.8 per cent of all tax dollars on past, present and future wars; the sound of Vice-President Agnew's outrage at Cornell students who, "wielding pipes and tire chains, beat a dormitory president into unconsciousness" (an event which the president of Cornell University himself assured him by urgent telegram was a figment of some speechwriter's imagination);[5] even the almost inaudible scream of would-be assassin Arthur Bremer's wish to have Donna Reed as his mother.[6]

---

[5] Both quotations from Albert Kahn, *The Unholy Hymnal* (London, 1972).
[6] *Time* magazine for May 29, 1972 carried a lengthy analysis of Arthur Bremer's *oeuvre,* including extracts from a high-school essay about families depicted on television, in the course of which the author fantasized Donna Reed as his mother.

The failure of the world of primary reality to yield to the all-embracing ethos of commercial publicity creates anxiety. That is why the consumer, the viewer, the voyeur of consumptive dreams is constantly urged to distrust his own physical experience of it. Suspended between the six o'clock news of what happens to other people and the situation comedy of his own life, he consumes the enormous output of journalists, writers, admen, producers, directors, cameramen and scientists in an effort—as continuous as television itself—to remain in orbit, slumped in a chair, surrounded by products, the trophies he brought back from earlier dreams.

Since the organization of public life is not yet perfect it straddles the two realities, condemned like some pioneer aircraft to land too frequently for comfort. Consequently there is enormous pressure on the wizards of media to develop techniques powerful enough to effect a permanent orbit, to iron out once and for all the mishaps that can shock and disturb the confident smile of power. Massive security precautions, law-and-order legislation, censorship of damaging news items, curbs on the power of the opposition, concealment of unpalatable facts, continuous rewriting of the rules of entry—all add up to a concerted effort to evade the uncertainties of democracy by abandoning primary reality altogether. The presentation of a therapeutic TV *realpolitik* with "simulations" of the President pulling off reassuring deals in Peking, Moscow and Hanoi is only part of it. A little work on Slater's "magic telegram" technique would show black militants sitting in a respectful semicircle at the feet of the Vice-President, or British miners sharing sandwiches with the Prime Minister on his yacht.[7]

Secondary reality has become so powerful and so seductive

[7] Or indeed newly released Vietnam P.O.W.'s lambasting the peace movement after six years in North Vietnamese jails. A triumph of secondary reality temporarily brought about by the administration in the early months of 1973.

and so woven into the fabric of Western consciousness that it is now more practical to plan the banishment of primary reality than to continue to pretend to be able to deal with the intractable horrors it presents.

In 1971, before the effective suppression of the United States Health, Education and Welfare Department's school bussing program, which was intended to integrate black and white children from ghetto and suburb, city authorities eager to prevent the hated measure from taking effect dreamed up numerous expedients to delay its onset. In Dallas the proposal was disturbingly predictive in its use of secondary-reality methods. Instead of a six-million-dollar bussing program to integrate its schools, it was proposed that a fifteen-million-dollar "community" television network should be installed linking schools from effectively segregated neighborhoods. Described by Dallas Schools Superintendent Nolan Estes as "The educational innovation of the decade," this project was enthusiastically endorsed by District Judge William Taylor. "What better way to start to foster integration," he is reported to have said,[8] "than for a child to be able to say: 'Hey, I saw you on television last week!' "

Unnecessary as this stratagem proved in practice, it reveals more about the real social destination of the "world community" of electronic communication than much current academic research on the subject. The notion that closed-circuit television, picturephones, remote medical diagnosis and telefactor gloves add up to a non-territorial, world-wide community structure is as naïve as the parallel dream of a future fun-factory to replace the work-factory of contemporary industrial society. Community structure as understood historically depended upon relationships which themselves derived from mutual obligations to ensure survival. In a world where individual survival depends on the *collapse* of mutual obliga-

[8] *Time,* August 16, 1971.

tion, where "security" will depend on the abandonment of primary reality itself, such terminology has become meaningless.

At present such of the dividing line between primary and secondary reality as remains still has a sharp edge. Sharp enough, as we have seen, to cut a personality, a policy, or a game to ribbons. In time this edge will disappear and we shall learn to accept that the public realm—winning, losing or performing—is over except as a paradigm, a system of analogies for trains of thought, a chess problem.

In this process the video-taped political career, the faked budget and foreign policy achievement, the bland denial and the amazing allegation will find their place. Not as scandalous aberrations, grave lapses from standards of public life established by antiquity, but as the unremarkable norms of government. Cynics may object that politics has always employed such methods, and that is true; the difference is that now they are grasped and accepted by a public which knowingly *prefers* them to any statement of real possibilities in a world whose real possibilities are running out fast. The factor of choice is important because it bypasses the whole question of repression. If the people *choose* a secondary-reality world of fake politics, simulated football games and surrogate *Grands Prix,* in preference to an exasperating reality of dispute and disqualification, bribery, sponsorship, and performances split by one thousandth of a second; then they are repressed no more than millions of young people are "exploited" by a recording industry whose products they purchase in such profusion.

Affluence has destroyed the sway of great ideas, and television has packaged and emasculated the impossible injustices, inequalities and corruptions of the rest of the world. Presented as they are, on television and in magazines, in the context of coke tins, cigar ads, and fashion features, these human disasters cannot inspire the populations of the wealthy nations of the West to rise up and redistribute the wealth and opportunity that remains accessible to humanity as a whole. To do so would be to sacrifice their own technologically reinforced consumer dream. They prefer to abandon the six o'clock news in favor of the commercials that surround it, just as they have already forsaken the real-world political pageant (spiced though it is with the chance of an assassination), in favor of the trusted fantasy of the television series.[9] News of the real world must already be carefully and attractively packaged. In San Francisco "KRON-TV Newshounds" wear giant bloodhound masks ("always hot on the scent of a story") and Channel 7 newsmen ride horses—"The magnificent 7 news gang rides out of the pages of the New West"—in desperate efforts to frame their bulletins in secondary-reality fun. In 1970, during the Palestine guerrilla hijacking of three planes, a TV news team paid £10,000 for an interview with a desert hostage—thereby partly financing their own news story. These extravagant efforts are largely in vain. A survey[10] carried out in San Francisco in 1971 which involved telephoning viewers directly after the evening news bulletin revealed that more than half of those who had heard or watched could not remember a single item in it. If news were a product pure and simple, its manufacturers would be bankrupt.

Secondary reality will triumph when a combination of *force majeure* and political realism finally convinces those in power that the servicing of the private lives of their subjects is their *sole* necessary duty and purpose. At that point the absurd morality which leads politicians to denounce consumer apathy and adolescent withdrawal—despite the fact that they have everything to gain from both—will collapse, and with it the expensive and counterproductive persecution of much of the

[9] Coverage of the 1972 Democratic convention in Miami was dominated by NBC, with 25 per cent of the national viewing audience. During the hours when NBC was broadcasting, ABC cornered a greater share of the audience (38 percent) with reruns of *Marcus Welby, Mod Squad* and *The Super.*
[10] Reported by Milton Shulman, London *Evening Standard,* February 9, 1972.

mechanism of privatization. When Vice-President Agnew denounced "the new morality" as "a cheap, easy rationale for doing whatever you damn please, wherever and however you want to do it,"[11] he conspicuously demonstrated a lack of understanding of the social disintegration which alone enables him, and men like him in Europe and America, to remain in power at all. Yet, as we have seen, such foolery is endemic in public life today, and it is not proof against a sudden access of secondary realism when occasion serves. The Chinese People's Republic, that pariah among nations within whose borders only five years ago Western newspaper correspondents had their heads shaved and their pet cats murdered, has played host to the American President and become a member of the United Nations at the expense of the old pretender to the mainland throne, Chiang Kai-Shek. The Soviet Union, allegedly poised for a quarter of a century on the brink of overwhelming Western Europe and burying the United States beneath tons of radioactive rubble, now emerges as a responsible super-power, considerate over the mining of North Vietnamese harbors and eager to sign an impressive charter of coexistence with her formerly implacable foe. Not that such accommodations have inhibited the ongoing development of weapon systems or the awarding of open-ended contracts for their production. The same President who as a "deeply committed pacifist" negotiated the Chinese and Russian *détente* and signed the strategic arms limitation agreement with the Soviet Union, simultaneously urged Congress to approve a 25 billion-dollar weapons program on the grounds that it would provide a "bargaining chip" for future negotiations along the same lines. What is the difference between an armaments program carried out under the nightmare urgency of a cold war, and an armaments program launched as a means of raising the stakes for future

---

[11] Part of speech by Spiro Agnew on being nominated "National Father of the Year" for 1972. *International Herald Tribune,* May 27 and 28, 1972.

triumphs of disarmament? Is it the "defense" system which pulls the roof in on top of the defenders, or the diplomatic achievement which has no discernible effect in the real world, which should be labeled "simulation"? The question raised at the beginning of this chapter can now be answered with some confidence. There is no effective difference between a simulated peace treaty in Hanoi and a television film of the real thing, simply because the real thing is no longer real. Secondary reality has made great strides in foreign policy since Gary Powers and the Bay of Pigs. The technique of suspended judgment has made simultaneous war and peace, poverty and affluence, honesty and deception, sickness and health, freedom and slavery, madness and sanity all possible at the same time *because they are no longer important.*

Thus when Henry Kissinger announced to the world in October 1972 that "Peace is at hand" after a decade of savage fighting in Vietnam, the world was prepared to accept Richard Nixon as the pacifist he always claimed to be. No matter if more than a third of the 56,000 Americans killed in the undeclared war died after his election in 1968 on a promise to end the conflict. No matter if half the 11,000,000 refugees in Vietnam were made homeless during the same period. No matter if between May and October 1972 he authorized air bombardment to the equivalent blast effect of ten Hiroshima bombs. No matter if in destroying food crops, poisoning forests, carrying out reprisals against civilians, seeding the clouds to cause torrential rains and massive flooding, experimenting with plastic anti-personnel bombs whose splinters are impossible to detect by X-ray, the American Air Force had committed war crimes according to the Geneva Convention rules for land warfare. Because the Nixon administration reduced American ground forces in Vietnam from over half a million to effectively none, efforts were made to have the President nominated for the Nobel Peace Prize even as he tripled the numbers of American soldiers, sailors and airmen actively engaged in the war from bases in Thailand, from Guam and from ships in the South China Sea.

Confronted with reduced draft calls and negligible casualties, the peace movement in the United States lost all political influence after 1971, even though the war itself was actually escalating in ferocity. With an instructive irony the bombing of North Vietnam was stepped up the day after the Berrigan brothers were acquitted of conspiracy to impede the prosecution of the war. Their protest, like those of draft card burners and leakers of officially incriminating documents, made no difference in the end because they had been overtaken by the technology, and the morality, of secondary reality.

George Orwell predicted that by 1984 war would have become peace. That has in one sense already happened because it is already easier to believe such an apparent contradiction than it is to give credence to the *real* contradiction evident in the traditional view. If war is hell, why do we continually endorse it? Not merely in Vietnam but in escalating defense budgets and the ceaseless development of nuclear weapons. Is it because we are all evil, or at least much more evil than we used to be? Or is it because we refuse to take our linguistic contradictions at their face value and thus ignore the evidence before our own eyes? To gasp with incredulity at the cynical duplicity of a President who promises "a new era of peace . . . and prosperity without war" the same day his air force drops 2,000 tons of bombs on the enemy is to misunderstand the depersonalization of the battlefield that another arm of the technology of privatization has made possible. There can be "a new era of peace" even at the rate of two Hiroshima-surrogates a month, just as there can be a form of social cohesion that is independent of any mutual obligation between people.

The twentieth century has seen an increasing remoteness in the conduct of its wars which exactly parallels the process of privatization that redistributed its peoples. From the invention of the airplane and the tank to the development of the inter-continental ballistic missile and the nuclear submarine the whole thrust of weapons development has been towards the substitution of technology for men, of firepower for combat. The enemy is reduced to a target, the target to a symbol, and the symbol itself connected to a trigger. The battlefield is vacated and surveyed from afar, the combatants are hidden deep in underground shelters; civilians have become the only visible targets, cities the only hostages. Under such conditions to claim that there is peace while there is still war—a war carried out automatically against unseen and unheard enemies —is a more defensible proposition than to claim that the population is wicked and their leaders mad. *When there are no casualties, no combatants, no victories and no defeats; when the war is endless and scarcely perceptible, then it has become figurative—like the "war" on crime, or the "war" on disease, or the "war" on poverty. Something you don't need to think about. No one need feel guilty about the war because nobody did it, no body, only machines.*

CHAPTER EIGHT

THE PRIVATE FUTURE: BATTLE OF TWO REALITIES

Primary

It's nine in the morning and raining hard. I've got a hangover and the photographer wants my nipples to stick out . . . I take a quick look at my boobs. They're still asleep and showing no signs of coming out to play . . . I put the dress on and take my knickers off. This makes me feel uncomfortable which gives me goosepimples which, in turn, pushes my nipples out. Good morning kids, I say. A quick squirt of hair lacquer on each nipple guarantees they will stay up for an hour . . .

Secondary

He took her to the edge of ecstasy and back again, keeping her hovering, sure of every move he made. Her breasts grew under his touch, swelling, becoming even larger and

firmer. She floated on a suspended plane, a complete captive
to his hands and body.[1]

This book so far has dwelt on several aspects of the emerging
pattern of privatization in Western society. First the contradiction between the present realities of community, family
and society and the received meaning of such words, and second with the idea that only a *myth* of community remains in
the West—a myth of such compelling power that it is not only
upheld in defiance of its obvious inapplicability, but used as
the basis for a "disease" theory of community decline. The
implementation of this theory, which is carried out in the teeth
of overwhelming evidence that this decline is passionately
desired, seeks to remedy it by arbitrary prohibitions and the
expansion of a bureaucracy of social engineers empowered to
make good the obvious deficiencies of what they do not see as
a transitional social organization. The myth of community
sickness also legitimizes the extinction of the remaining areas
of public life by subjecting them to environmental terrorism in
the guise of "security." In this way the traditional forms of
Western political democracy, like the competitive tradition
enshrined in sport and entertainment, and—as we shall see—
employment, are increasingly subjected to pressures which
threaten their destruction as manifestations of an authentic
public realm.

The perverse result of these massive efforts to "save" a concept of social obligation already obliterated by the success of
individual materialism, is that the process of privatization is
accelerated by the increasing uninhabitability of what is left of
the public realm. As a consequence the dependence of individuals on the compensating technology of private affluence

[1] Quotations at head of chapter: Vicky Hodge, the London *Sunday Mirror,*
June 4, 1972. Jackie Collins, *The World is Full of Married Men* (London,
1969).

—as exemplified by consumer goods—has increased to the point where the *real* basis of social stability has become paradoxically dependent on continued progress towards autonomy through increased consumption. Within the breast of the private citizen today lurks not a yearning for an older, simpler pattern of community obligations, but a desperate desire for a commodity-induced nirvana to obliterate fears of a future seemingly blocked by insoluble crises in the form of overpopulation, resource exhaustion, pollution or nuclear war.

If the goal system of Western affluence breaks down, what lies beneath it is not a renewed sense of community through scarcity, but an absolute social collapse without the security of interpersonal and inter-family support. Affluence is *vital* to the social organization of the Western world because it has supplanted all the old systems of mutual obligation. The political behavior of consumers, including the young, over recent years has confirmed their refusal to entertain any idea of voluntarily relinquishing the trappings of private consumption in the interests of a more equitable society.

Confused by a vocabulary that does not enable him to understand his absolute dependence on those consumer goods which he affects to regard as of lesser importance than his personal relationships, the private citizen of the West is beginning to develop instead a willfully sustained system of therapeutic deceptions termed in this book secondary reality. He uses this secondary reality as a means of escape from contradictions which, through the ubiquity of media "news," are seen as insoluble but impossible to ignore. To face a futureless future he *relies* on self-deception, and that self-deception is itself fed and developed by recording and simulating technologies which have formalized it and given it the appearance of truth. The conflict between this technologically reinforced pursuit of a personalized therapy of fantasy, and the seemingly intractable realities of the real world, forms the subject of this final chapter.

The triumph of mass media as the purveyors of secondary reality reflects the refusal of the people of the West to accept the implications of the collapse of community. The fragmentation of society *is* a reality, but the priceless distraction of erotic and sensory fantasy products and services conceals it. Those artists and intellectuals who resisted the absorption of their images and insights into the vast pleasure machine of commercial advertising and entertainment have paid for their integrity by finding themselves recast as stern-faced moralists, as remote from the ideas and aspirations of the masses as is Herbert Marcuse's concept of a "liberation" from affluence. Today the true descendant of Rimbaud's "I" who is "someone else" is not the poet living on welfare or the student revolutionary, but the worker offering his life to a meaningless job because it pays off in the fantasy reward of the endless consumer dream. Today the true descendants of the pioneer Surrealist Jacques Vaché (who reputedly spent much of the First World War frequenting bars in the city of Nantes dressed as a fighter pilot, wearing numerous unearned decorations and boasting of outrageous exploits), are neither revolutionaries nor artists but the millions of subtly mutated spectators who emerge from the cinema clad in the fantasy identities of gangsters, whores, secret agents, hippies, revolutionaries and spies. Consumer society has become a form of barter for dreams, and nothing in it is more surrealistic than the practice of work itself: no one more dedicated to the relentless servicing of his "other self" than the worker. Compared to any consumer the artist has become a monk, the revolutionary a fakir lying on a bed of nails.

As long ago as 1936 the economist Maynard Keynes explained the fundamentally surrealistic nature of employment in any capitalist society by expounding the case for public works in the following striking way:[2]

---

[2] J. M. Keynes, *General Theory of Employment, Interest and Money* (Macmillan, London, 1936).

If the Treasury were to fill old bottles with bank-notes, bury them at suitable depths in disused coal mines which are then filled up to the surface with town rubbish, and leave it to private enterprise on well-tried principles of *laissez-faire* to dig the notes up again (the right to do so being obtained, of course, by tendering for leases of the note-bearing territory), there need be no more unemployment and, with the help of the repercussions, the real income of the community, and its capital wealth also, would probably become a good deal greater than it actually is. It would indeed be more sensible to build houses and the like; but if there are political and practical difficulties in the way of this, the above would be better than nothing.

In the event, as several commentators have pointed out, munitions production proved a good substitute for buried bottles of money, and ways have since been found to turn the construction of houses into something equally profitable. But the irrational basis of consumer economics remains and has indeed permeated every area of production. Today, with the technology of secondary reality securely entrenched at the heart of the *meaning* of consumption, the marketing not merely of products but of work itself has fallen under the domination of the bizarre and the arcane, becoming interpretable and meaningful only by means of fantasies of personal distraction. Careers, jobs, advertising for jobs, surviving jobs, and being rewarded for jobs, all have become adjuncts to a grand and realizable fantasy. Consider these advertisements:

Hello Claire. Come in and have a chat . . . We've a young crowd working here on a wide range of jobs . . . Underwriting, claims, personnel and many more. We'll give you a proper office training . . . There's a fabulous staff restaurant—and terrific afterwork activities including drama-club, ten-pin bowling, swimming and horse riding . . .

Bit worried about leaving home? So was I. I didn't have much of a trade in civilian life. It was humdrum—no future. I wanted to

get around! . . . I decided I'd like the RAF police. I trained in
basic police work and got my stripes, then I volunteered for dog
handling. I enjoyed that! I learned to drive too—cars and motor
bikes. And I've certainly got around. I've been in Aden and Cyprus
as well as Britain. Then I learned special investigation. That's
mostly my job these days.

Graduate in philosophy aged 23 years. This very attractive young
lady, after gaining an honours degree, is working as a Zookeeper.
She would be quite happy to continue doing this but the work is
only seasonal. She is finding it hard to get a job, as people are
wary of her degree. She is ultra-reliable, very keen to learn anything and work hard at it at a salary of about £18 per week. She is
a bargain for anyone who will overlook her degree and give her a
chance to prove herself.

The first of these advertisements, for a large insurance company, mentions three types of work and five types of amusement (if we include eating in the fabulous staff canteen). The
second, for the Royal Air Force, represents service life as a
combination of foreign holidays, playing with exciting equipment and becoming a sort of secret agent. The third, put out
by a small office staff agency, attempts to sell a university
graduate as an *amusement* who is also "very attractive."
    Fantasy plays a different but equally dominant role in the
actual execution of work. In offices such as the one Claire is
being invited to work in, the turnover in junior staff alone
belies the attractions listed in the advertisement. As a brochure
for a "Functional music service" puts it:

You've seen her come, you've seen her go, what was her name?
Mabel? June? Ann? [No, it was Claire, actually] The turnover of
staff in your office is so regular you could get used to it—if it
wasn't so expensive and so inconvenient. You're not unusual, most
employers can expect an office staff turnover of 50% or beyond
. . . Staff leave because they become bored. Same office, same boss,
same work, the only changing factor is the constant arrival and

departure of other junior staff—for a change, they change. Muzak is an effective answer to boredom. Muzak provides the one varying factor in an otherwise unvarying environment . . . At the time of the day when an employee's morale normally falls, Muzak provides more stimulating music.

The answer is clear. If the drama club, ten-pin bowling, swimming and horse riding fail, then it's time for music. Background music that can act as an aural prop for almost any kind of fantasy existence. For the three-quarters of a million "half-trained gipsy clerical workers"[3] who in Britain switch from job to job because it is "the only changing factor," the pursuit of private fantasies fed by advertising represents the only meaningful aspect of employment.

The machinery of electronic data processing, like the machinery of private consumption, decreases dependent human contact and cooperation. As with the TV watcher, so with the punch-card operator. As with the driver, so with the audiotypist: an endless, private world of fantasy behind a façade of mechanical repetition.

In the Services too, when recruits tire of dog-handling and driving cars and motor bikes, there are signs that the tentacles of consumer fantasy reach in towards them. In February 1972 a bankruptcy hearing revealed that nearly one hundred British soldiers from a barracks at Aldershot had become agents for a company selling property bonds. The soldiers had bought discharges in order to pursue their new careers and one had become a deputy marketing director before bankrupting himself in an effort to increase sales.

Production-line work, which is more closely matched to the motor rhythms of machines than any other, is made bearable only by the close relationship between the consumer rewards which accompany long hours of overtime, and the fantasies

---

[3] A term used by the general secretary of the Clerical and Administrative Workers Union to describe temporary office staff.

which can be sustained and developed during those hours. Repeatedly carrying out simple operations, sometimes for years at a stretch, the line worker is able to fuse the patiently fostered hallucinations that enable him to survive interminable hours of labor into the pattern of imagery presented to him at other times by newspapers, television, advertising and entertainment in general. It is by this means that he is able to ignore the fact that his attempt to improve his standard of living by means of endless work is self-defeating. The hours he works may wipe out his social life, but because he is on line to the consumer fantasy system in a sense that is probably only also true of housewives who share the same extreme isolation, this loss is compensated for in another area of life altogether. As long as his brief hours of leisure are pumped full of the imagery that is the raw material of his fantastic dreams, this internalized system of rewards remains intact. The very fact that the production-line worker does not have *time* to exhaust the potential of those consumer trinkets that he can afford is an important factor in retaining his enthusiasm for them: his life is passed in dreams that are no less real than the apparent occupation of his working hours.

There are nine men all told who work on our line, and each one is a character, an individual in his own right. My work comes to me in a completely automatic way, in the gestures of automation. With a rag wrapped around my eyes I could still do it, and could do dozens before I realized that I had done any at all. But underneath all this my mind never stops working. It lives by itself. Some call it dreaming, and if so, I am dreaming all day long, five days a week. The whole bench dreams like this. *It is a galley of automatons locked in dreams.*[4]   (Emphasis supplied)

[4] From "On the Line" in *Work: Twenty Personal Accounts.* Ed. Ronald Fraser. (Pelican, London.) The articles originally appeared in *New Left Review.*

Whether the dreams themselves be erotic, Adlerian or merely opportunistic is not at this stage important. The worker quoted above later mentions dreams of being an artist, a gravedigger, a hired assassin and a revolutionary. Vauxhall workers interviewed by a reporter from a daily newspaper confessed to dreaming of houses—"I don't give a damn what I do as long as I get a house"[5]—and cars. Unable to grasp the importance of another manifestation of this fantasy system, the reporter himself appeared shocked that the company should pay workers to act as runners to place bets for production-line men. rather than suffer continual absenteeism for this reason.

Housework shares the isolation and fantasy of the production line. A housewife who describes her life as "one long system, cleaning the living room on Mondays, the kitchen on Tuesdays and so on until Friday when it's shopping day"[6] will also confess to daydreams of being a GoGo dancer, of meeting the Queen, of going on long, tropical holidays. She will play bingo for prizes of canned food, dance alone to the programs of favorite DJ's and enthusiastically play the simple stamp trading games that marketing people devise to strengthen brand loyalties. Her identification with the characters in TV serials shows the same patiently developed perfection as does the hallucinatory liberation of the line worker. Such viewers protest in their thousands when a character is killed off or written out. More directly even than TV series, giveaway quiz programs feed her consumer dreams by endlessly rerunning the expressions of delight and disbelief that attend the award of the tape recorder, the fondue set, the electric frying pan, the color TV, in response to simple questions or feats of memory.[7]

[5] "As Long As You Get There on Time, They Don't Care How Lazy You Are at Work," *Daily Mail,* May 5, 1971.
[6] "The Housewife Who Had Her Day," London *Sunday Times Magazine,* July 19, 1970.
[7] Daytime television in the United States is dominated by such programs as "Dating Game," "Let's Make a Deal" and so on. In Britain "Sale of the Century" and "The Generation Game" exemplify the same format.

The expressions are important because the basis of the nirvana of private consumption *is* fantastic. It *is* better to give than to receive, and many a football pool coupon is filled in with the expressions of gratitude on the faces of the winners' beneficiaries in mind—even though the chance of winning is lower than the chance of being murdered.

It should not be thought that this pattern of fantasy-satisfaction is limited to working-class people in the sense that term is normally employed. The same process of dislocated reward operates throughout Western society. In separating out the elements of existence so that some become wholly rewarding while others are consciously obliterated no matter how great a proportion of his time they take up, the worker merely acts out one reflection of the system of fragmentation that is central to all the manifestations of Western materialism. Others are to be seen in activities as disparate as executive training schemes and factory farming. The latter in particular, with its ability to use the physiological processes of nutrition and reproduction in animals to the exclusion of the wholeness of their existence, amounts to a paradigm for the whole process.

In the world of the business executive—although in business it is well known that *everybody* calls himself an executive—images of status and achievement predominate. Questioned in a motivational study carried out by a leading financial newspaper one enthusiastic company man suggested that the paper should advertise by illustrating "a brisk-looking man of about 45 years getting out of his car with the paper under his arm and walking towards the firm's entrance to give a feeling of business and progress." Structural in such a vision is the idea of *achievement,* which is after all supposed to be the chief factor differentiating the life of the executive from that of the housewife or the production-line worker. Yet what is the reality of the working life of the executive "achiever," or indeed of the architect, the TV producer, the "creative" advertising man, the doctor or any of the other brisk-looking men of 45 years who populate advertisements? According to an outspoken tutor at the London Business School:[8]

The problems of the achiever are only beginning. In large organizations and where tasks are complex, vital communications are lateral and face to face. Many people are involved. Objectives cease to be clear-cut and are frequently conflicting. Risks are no longer personal but collective. Time-lapses between action and outcome increase. Absolute standards disappear. *Notions like success and failure merge into meaninglessness.* Even the engineers who designed the Concorde would pause to answer if asked whether or not their project is a success. It is frequently impossible for us to evaluate personal contributions and performances. In short, there is an absence of that tangible feedback on which the achiever depends. These are crisis conditions for the achiever and they pertain to the whole of industry and particularly to large organizations.   (Emphasis supplied.)

Despite the large-scale recruitment of graduates into business with such lures as Job Enrichment, Management by Objectives and continuous assessment for promotion, four-fifths of a recent newspaper survey among professionals revealed that they felt under-employed in their work. Management studies themselves are but desperate attempts to rediscover or fake the "wholeness" of jobs that have long since distintegrated into fragmentary, disconnected activities without beginnings, middles or ends. The real achievements of the executive's career are to be found—like those of the production-line worker, the humble soldier, the housewife—in the world of fantasy that income derived from work can provide in the private realm. In a serialized account of her life with Clive Raphael, the property developer, his widow recorded that the young London tycoon (who drove a white Rolls Royce with

[8] Denis Pym, "On the Gospel of Work," *Architectural Association Quarterly,* London, Autumn 1971.

Philadelphia license plates) always maintained a pretense that his frequent business trips abroad were important diplomatic missions or espionage operations. "Every summer he would disappear for several weeks, saying he was going on a tuning-up weapons course because there were dangerous jobs ahead."[9]

It is the role and responsibility of the rich worker to act out the fantasies of the poor worker, and if that involves Philadelphia license plates and secret missions overseas we should not be surprised—for only those so poor as to be compelled to live in the public realm entirely, lack the basic domestic ingredients for the maintenance of fantasies about themselves.[10] For them, the homeless, the vagrants and the alcoholics, there is only the put up or shut up of delusions of grandeur which have to be *proved* if they are not to be derided.

Work itself is not the linking factor between the various classes of employed persons, but the world of secondary reality which sustains their fantasies is shared by all of them. The present status of employment is artificial in that it merely masks a pursuit of fantasy that is thought to be impossible by any other means, but in the course of the evolution of the private future this situation will change rapidly. Already official statistics indicate that the process of *withdrawal* from employment may be more significant in the long run than widely publicized disputes between organized labor and employers over pay and conditions.

In the early spring of 1972, workers at the General Motors Lordstown, Ohio, facility producing the Vega subcompact on a new automated assembly line began deliberately misassembling the cars. The management reacted by refusing to allow overtime for repairs, sending line workers home instead when jobs backed up in the repair shop. The result was ab-

---

[9] "Nudes Will Penny Tells it All," *News of the World,* November 19, 1972.
[10] In Britain under current regulations, a dwelling is necessary for the regular payment of welfare benefits. If a claimant has no address, collecting benefit is deliberately made difficult as a precaution against fraud.

senteeism climbing to 20 per cent of the work force, a complaints list twice as long as the preceding year, and finally a three-week strike which ended only when GM agreed to slow the assembly line to its previous, preautomation rate—thereby losing the productivity advantage which their heavy investment in numerically controlled machine tools had promised.

The name Lordstown passed into common management parlance, not merely as a defeat, but as a code word for a new phenomenon. Lordstown was significant for four reasons. First, because the workers concerned were young—average age below twenty-five. Second, because the assembly line was not only automated to an unprecedented degree, but the Vega itself specially designed for automated assembly. Third, because the strike was called during a period of high unemployment by a union already impoverished as the result of a previous nine-week strike. Fourth, and most important of all, because the men were not striking for more pay or fringe benefits but as a protest against "dehumanized work."

Lordstown sounded an alarm bell for management in America that the "alarm industry" is at present amplifying and extending into the same reaches of paranoia that accommodate antidrug legislation. To the fear of drugs at work ("today the colleges, tomorrow the corporations")[11] is added the fear of anarchy on the assembly line. "Overeducated young people with high expectations and little patience may give you a lot of Lordstowns," *Business Week* reported Professor Ivor Berg of Columbia University as saying six months later.[12] "Some may settle down, others may respond with alcoholism, revolution, or just apathy." Whichever one they choose, we can be sure that "job enlargement," "flexible hours," "task

[11] For a searching analysis of the role of the alarm industry in America see Harrison M. Trice and Paul M. Roman, *Spirits and Demons at Work: Alcohol and Other Drugs on the Job.* (Cornell University Press, Ithaca, N.Y., 1972).

[12] *Business Week,* September 23, 1972.

force" work, even wage incentives can no longer offer an effective antidote. Nothing in the managerial box of tricks can ever restore the unquestioning servitude of the past once it is lost. And the sum of all available evidence indicates that it is indeed lost and gone forever.

Surveys of work attitudes among U.S. college students (of whom there will be an unemployable surplus of nearly two million by 1980) indicate that whereas five years ago half of them did not object to the future prospect of being "bossed around" on the job, by 1971 this proportion had sunk to one third. Among young workers, although positive data on the growth of absenteeism, sabotage and high turnover rates is jealously guarded by major employers, all the evidence adduced by the 1972 HEW report "Work in America" indicates that the same spirit of resistance to the very basis of *employment*—though not of consumption—is growing at a rapid rate. The report parenthesized the fears of governments and employers everywhere when it noted "One wonders what will happen when the children of today's open classroom, who have been taught to set their own goals and plan their own schedules, enter the workforce."[13]

The late twentieth-century discovery that work is absurd and intrinsically unrewarding is in reality nothing more than a rediscovery. It was clear not only to the increasingly admired aboriginal occupants of the North American and other colonized continents, but even to the peasants and smallholders of eighteenth-century Europe, men who ultimately *chose* to be drawn into the process of industrial manufacture that led in time to the birth of consumer societies. From the beginning the rewards of industrial work were separate from the exercise of it, indeed it was the first work to be totally recompensed in the abstract currency of money instead of in

---

[13] "Work in America," Report of a Special Task Force to the Secretary of Health, Education and Welfare (The M.I.T. Press, Cambridge, Mass., 1973).

goods or services. Industrial work triumphed as a means of fulfilling dreams, dreams which scarcely existed until the miracle of mass production made them more accessible by far to the populations of the West than the older vision of heaven had ever been, if only because the democratization of work created social envy—the idea that anyone could obtain what anyone else possessed. The peculiar crisis of motivation in work today consists not only in the fact that it must still be carried out in the intractable public world of primary reality while its reward is to be found in the private pursuit of power, pleasure and orgasm, but in the tantalizing possibility of a world without work in which these same rewards could be retained. The *contingency* of work has been destroyed by technology. Irrespective of the hours he works or the job he holds, today's worker already half lives in a world of successive, technically repeatable pleasures of repeated orgasms technically immunized against consequences; of potentially endless, chemically sustained voyages into nirvana.

The products themselves defeat work. They do not violently overthrow it, but they steadily undermine it. They do not deny it but they mock it. Work today has ceased to be serious in all but its anachronistic role as a passport to the wonderland of private fantasy. This paradox grasped, the future of employment as a route to private pleasure can be mapped out by analogy.

Imagine the worker as a drug addict—by this time it should be clear that the term "worker" is being used in its broadest possible sense. He works for money, an abstraction which Friedrich Engels described in terms wholly consonant with this emotive parable as "The commodity of commodities, that which holds all other commodities hidden in itself, the magic power which can change at will into everything desirable and desired."[14] With the aid of this abstraction he purchases goods

---

[14] Friedrich Engels, *The Origin of the Family, Private Property and the State,* International Publishers (Chicago, 1902; first published Zurich, 1884).

and achieves a high-status self-image. Since status in a consumer society incorporates elements of fantasy, the substitution of a drug which induces fantasy for commodities which confer status will create no confusion. Thus under present circumstances we can say that the worker (addict) buys commodities (drugs) which induce status (fantasy). Clearly, for reasons given in earlier chapters, the worker's desire for fantasy escalates in proportion to increasing availability, which is itself guaranteed by consumer-product evolution (drug development). The worker is consequently subjected to three temptations to which he must yield. First, he must increase his income in order to buy more drugs. Second, he must supplement his supply of drugs by trying to obtain them direct. Third, he must try to turn his work into a drug experience—in effect to have his addiction rechristened "work." He must either become a rich drug addict, a criminal drug addict, or a famous drug addict. The only alternative is to kick his habit altogether by espousing the cause of socialist revolution—and why should he do that when the shops are bulging with all the drugs he needs?

The gradual triumph of all three temptations will shape the social pattern of future non-employment. First, the demand for increased income (which grows in proportion to inflation in the economies of the West) will in turn lead to more and more *ostensible* conflicts between organized labor and the attempts of governments to mop up excess purchasing power by means of wage restraint. In the course of this developing struggle work itself will assume an even more peripheral role against a background of increasing automation, increasing unemployment and a growing rhetoric of militancy on all sides. Second, the tendency to short-cut the pursuit of fantasy by dispensing with the least essential element of the work-money-consumption cycle will become prominent in a number of related ways. Crimes, particularly robbery, tax evasion,

petty theft, fraud, embezzlement, blackmail and extortion will
steadily increase along lines already evident.[15]

At the same time a steadily increasing proportion of the
population will drop out of the employment system, either
absolutely—through becoming unemployable[16]—or through
the disintegration of the relationships which make their work
possible. Who, for instance, will replace the housewife, whose
personalized services sustain the male worker, when perfect
contraception and the ideology of personal liberation have
percolated down from their present middle-class home; when
equal pay and the accelerating impermanence of marriage
have separately undermined the old ethics of duty? The simultaneous increase in part-time, non-productive and therapeutic
employment such as is currently offered by the service and
entertainment industries, as well as the growth of self-employ-

---

[15] This obvious but usually ignored motivation for crime was clearly enun-
ciated by a witness to the notorious Fulham scrap-yard killings of 1968. "If
I work all my life, the top I'll get is £20 a week. I'm working till I'm 60-
odd—what have I got to show for it? I want my kids to have the best
possible education they can. I really think that if I could find the right
opening I could go straight. *But if you're working for somebody, you're
nettled from the start."* More generally the recorded increase in shoplifting
with annual losses to the retail trade of £300,000,000, the gross increase
in criminal prosecutions of 1,300 per cent since 1900 (Britain's population has
increased by 47 per cent), the £150,000,000 lost annually through tax-
dodging and the £10,000,000 outstanding in unpaid fines attest to the
emergence of a dishonesty which is only new in that it is socially acceptable.
A Kilburn housewife wrote to the London *Daily Mirror* in March 1972:
"What would you do with neighbours like mine? Both work in factories.
One offers me bottles of scent and soap saying 'Ask no questions.' When I
refuse she throws them over the wall into my garden and laughs. I put them
in the dustbin and then worry in case someone finds them when investi-
gating the pilfering. The other neighbour puts tights and panties in my shopping bag. When I put them back she calls me a "mug" and says 'You'll
never get on.'"

[16] A direct result of the alarm-industry inspired screening methods used by
almost all large-scale employers in the United States has been an increasing
number of persons disbarred from regular employment by criminal records,
political affiliations, even personal appearance.

ment, workers' control and the proliferation of bureaucracies of surveillance, police forces and auxiliary security corps will also have their effect. More important still will be the increasing proportion of populations whose incomes will be dependent on government allowances and subsidies—for reasons we have discussed, their impetus to work harder in the pursuit of wealth will have disappeared completely.

With a political process that is already merely a front for a universal servicing and supply system for the private realm; with a culture of public spectacle that is already dissolving into a miniaturized technology of private nirvana; with a social prognosis that is already fraught with predictable public doom from nuclear war, population growth, resource exhaustion or pollution; with a pattern of social cohesion already dependent on *separation* rather than combination; with an ethic of labor and reward already overturned by glaring evidence of its failure to deliver dreams fast enough and far enough; with a population paralyzed by its awful, incontrovertible knowledge of how impossible the future of the Western world really is— only secondary reality, only fantasy, only madness, only *privacy* can still offer an open door. Only our matchless consumer imagery, our cinematic, televisual, electronic technology of the simulation of life can enable us to pass through it.

The third temptation, to turn work into fantasy, to become a famous drug addict, means in effect to reunite those aspects of social behavior which in Western societies are at present proscribed with the mainstream of private consumption. What is now regarded as aberrant, antisocial and criminal will come to be seen as the logical pattern of development of a materialistic culture of private affluence. Such a process of reintegration is inevitable if Western culture is to survive a future that in historical terms is no future at all. The very absence of any prognosis apart from increasing environmental terrorism and the threat of ecological doom will cause a rapid lowering of horizons. As the foreseeable lifespan of society shortens to parity with the lifespan of the individual human being, demand for a cheaper and faster nirvana will drive first the dispossessed and subsidized poor, and later the orthodox suburban consumer himself, into the arms of the drug culture—which will in turn acknowledge its long-denied parentage. The so-called counter-culture, itself born out of the teenage market created by affluence, will reveal itself for what it really is, not the vanguard of a new sense of community, but the logical product of the collapse of the old.

Today, despite propaganda to the contrary that is itself a product of the community myth, there is no emerging culture that is not ultimately subject to the same constraints and hypnotized by the same lures as its predecessor. The great fiasco of the teenage vote, like the myth of revolution without popular support, clearly demonstrates the private destiny of liberated youth, not its unification into a political and ideological force capable of overthrowing the basis of mass consumption.

Ideology is instrumental, and an ideology of revolution serves well in developing countries where the hope of prosperity by any other means was all but extinguished by economic colonization. In the affluent West the ideology of youth revolt is also an instrument, devised to frighten and combat those who illogically proscribe some patterns of fantasy indulgence at the expense of others. The emergence of the "counter-culture" from the bosom of consumer society guarantees that the revolutionary notion of "millions of kids" who will fight to free their leaders jailed at the end of the Chicago conspiracy trial[17] is as chimerical as the "final election in the sky"[18] invoked by Hubert Humphrey, the political leader of another generation. The leaders of the Yippies, like the leaders of the old political parties, are blinded by forms of secondary reality that prevent them from clearly seeing the realities of their own time. Humphrey with his desire to be

[17] As predicted by Jerry Rubin at the time.
[18] See above, p. 132.

vindicated by divine intervention, and Rubin with his historical vision of an avenging mob, are both anachronisms. Commenting on the outcome of the 1972 Presidential election, when for the first time twenty million young persons aged between eighteen and twenty-one were able to vote, Rubin said, "White Christian America is committing suicide. They may win the election but they will lose the world."[19] Where were the "millions of kids" on that occasion? Surely even they, surly and lazy as they are, would have risen up to vote to *save the world*. The fact that they did not confirms not only that the Youth International Party had steadfastly *refused* to "be something more than a market for the record and clothing and dope business"[20] since its inception in 1967, it proves more tragically that the counter-culture no less than the political establishment of the Left has failed to understand the process of privatization which dominates the *whole* of Western society. The failure of the pop festival movement even more clearly illustrates the same crucial failure to understand what is wanted and what is not.

In the summer of 1969 at the apogee of the festival movement, half a million young people gathered at Woodstock, New York, and constituted briefly the tenth largest city in the United States. This counter-culture army—as large as the force sent by Napoleon to conquer Russia—survived for only a few days, supplied in the main by the helicopters and trucks of its establishment enemies, whose security forces had been overwhelmed by the unexpected numbers. At the height of this unprecedented event the Yippie leader Abbie Hoffman seized a microphone to announce that the festival was meaningless as long as the manager of MC5 (a Detroit rock band) was still in jail on a marijuana charge. This logical attempt to draw the attention of the army to the more serious issues

[19] BBC New York coverage of the U.S. Presidential election, November 7, 1972.
[20] Gene Marine, "Chicago" (*Rolling Stone,* April 2, 1970).

that confronted it was summarily dealt with. The guitarist Pete Townsend beat him off the stage with his instrument, leading an anonymous commentator to joke later, "That's the relationship between politics and rock."[21]

The joke was on them all. Despite the extensive plans made at the festival organizers' conference in New Mexico that October, the movement never again achieved the same impact, nor the same potential political power. For the future, in Europe as well as America, the organization of festivals was dogged by those very forces of fragmentation and affluence that over the preceding century had turned the older cities of both continents inside out, and spread their occupants thinly over new suburban areas. The instant urbanism of the festival proved no more able to resist the suburbanism of privatized societies than had the ancient urbanism of the preindustrial world.

In the following year the festival dream of a new culture was sucked down and dissipated by the disintegrating realities of the old culture of which it was an integral part. Condemned to old-style finance and forced to conform to increasingly stringent security regulations, it fell prey to financial catastrophes, not in subsequent cases averted by the film rights windfall that saved Woodstock. Irritating stipulations over hygiene (based upon impossible requirements inherited from static entertainment facilities) caused increasing friction between organizers and the authorities they were obliged to placate in order to obtain land. Finally a formula was devised by opponents of the gatherings whereby the endemic drug-taking came to be used as the same kind of lever for the dismemberment of the festivals as slum conditions had provided for the dismemberment of the cities. In five years the economy of the new instant cities was obliterated by the same pattern of legislation as had taken a hundred years to decentralize their

[21] Jerry Hopkins, *Festival!* (Collier-Macmillan, New York, 1970).

predecessors. "Drug abuse," like "slums," came to be defined as an evil which legitimized the extinction of the pattern of community that accompanied it. The Woodstock army, demoralized by the Altamont tragedy, its territory and supplies held hostage by treacherous financiers, its troops disorganized and dispersed, surrendered to the enemy without a fight. The terms of the surrender established conditions for the conduct of future campaigns which could not be met without sacrificing every principle on which the counter-culture imagined itself to be based. The "millions of kids" who had briefly appeared on the field of Woodstock, drifted away to smoke their joints and listen to their music in basement rooms or remote settlements. Their leaders, like the Indian chiefs of a century before, smoked cigars, had their photographs taken, and were absorbed.[22]

The fact that music and drugs, and not revolution, assembled the counter-culture army to begin with was no accident. Both are key components in the technology of privatization, which can be relied upon to sever the bonds of community with laser-like speed irrespective of their composition. Music and drugs, like cars, houses and freezers, are part of the wonderfully complex Western system of techno-therapy which converts the pain of isolation into the onanistic pleasure of autonomy. It does this by separating out even the elements of consciousness so that the vicious circle whereby spiritual isolation and terror act directly upon the motor functions of behavior is broken. We are not prisoners like rats in a maze because we have ceased to act as whole rats: by an enormous system of chemistry and technique we have become bits of personalities linked only by a music which must never stop— because if it does the pain will be absolute and instantaneous.

[22] In November 1972 the Youth International Party repudiated the rights of Abbie Hoffman and Jerry Rubin to act as spokesmen for the party on the grounds that they had been calling off or quelling useful and necessary demonstrations as well as using their status in the party for personal gain.

In this way all the trinkets of our technology, from the heroin needle to the long-playing record, are geared to keeping bits of ourselves alive in isolation. Divided we stand, united we fall. Our medicine is continual surgery between the parts of ourselves, and in that sense the drugs, the cars, the mortgages, the police and the dope fiends are all together in the same voluntary concentration camp.[23] And it is as occupants of one single camp that all the citizens of the consumer societies of the West will pursue their own private means of escape from the terrors of the public future—an escape facilitated, like the collapse of community itself, by the electronic incarnation of secondary reality.

As has been suggested before in this book, the growth and development of communications media into a network that embraces almost every person in the Western world can be seen as symbiotic with the whole process of privatization. Without the camera, the telephone, the gramophone, popular newspapers, the cinema, radio, television and the tape recorder, there would be no suburbs, no demand for single-person housing, no instrumental counter-culture created to politicize demand for the liberation of irrationally denied pleasures. Without the limitless ingenuity of media technology, without the panorama, the close-up, the face shot, the jump cut, the freeze frame, the pixilation, the zoom and the slow-motion replay, the magic of the old public realm might not have succumbed to scrutiny and exploitation. Politics might not have ossified into a sterile technique, and sport might have evaded the commercial sponsorship and stop-watch dissection that has turned it into a futile succession of dead-heats and

[23] *Rolling Stone* for August 6, 1970, featured a survey of festivals with many random interviews, few of the subjects of which came up with big *cultural* interpretations of the events themselves. Most were cynical about the concepts of music, love and peace. One eighteen-year-old girl even hoped that when the plastic people finally put all the hippies in concentration camps, they would have the sense to provide music and dope as well.

riots. Entertainment itself might have remained a matter of circuses and marching bands, Grand Operas and historical pageants. As it is, centrally controlled broadcasting media, aided by a ubiquitous and prurient press, have succeeded in driving the spokesmen of the public realm into a cabalistic conspiracy concealed beneath layers of perfectly learned secondary-reality technique. The unflappable politician, the endlessly smiling celebrity, the sportsman who is also a minor commercial empire, are all products of the seizure and homogenization of the public realm by media—just as the football riot and the rigged Le Mans victory are products of its extinction of the possibility of real competition.

But the process of media scrutiny is endless and endlessly fertile. The zoom lens that can pick out a face across a crowded street, a pair of eyes, a mouth, presages the scrutiny and celebration of *private* as opposed to public spectacle. The cameras have switched from the mummified corpse of the public realm to the infinitely more exciting pursuit of the essence of private behavior. We have become bored already by the perfection of a girl's smile, by the beauty of her hair photographed against the sun, tiny instants turned into clichés by the repetition of a thousand television commercials. But that is only the beginning of the love affair between the camera and the private future.

Today, success in the world of entertainment is already conditional upon what is generally called the "sacrifice" of private life. Popular magazines and newspapers are filled with ritual interviews in which the victims of wealth, fame and public exposure describe the "pressures" of life at the top. "I don't think many people could have lived through what I have," said Judy Garland[24] a few months before she died. "When I get home at night, I'm like a zombie, I just sit," said Marc Bolan in an interview. "Yesterday I burst out crying for no reason at

[24] Judy Garland, "My Agony," *News of the World,* June 29, 1969.

all. I often get brought down."[25] Yet the basis of this feeling of horror and loss is seldom if ever closely defined. Perhaps it is objectively indefinable. "I didn't ask to be a legend. How does a legend behave? Are there any rules to follow? Nobody has written a book about it," complained Judy Garland. And she was right. The life of an entertainment legend is incomprehensible because what is scrutinized and loved, what millions of people pay to see is the unprogrammable, indefinable essence of the private person who agrees to live in public—not to live a public life, *but to live in public* the life that is otherwise hidden away in the impenetrable otherness of other people. The achievement of the recording media has been to find a way to expose this privacy, to examine it and glorify it above all public things. A star is a private person living in a glass booth. A public career is a triumph of privacy, and the uncertainty of the star as to what he or she actually *does* to merit such attention is nothing more than the uncertainty and confusion every individual feels about his own meaning. Thus the idea that nude theater and public sex mark the end of privacy is diametrically wrong; they represent its *celebration.* When Judy Garland turned up an hour and a half late for a performance, only to be shouted at and pelted with breadsticks, cigarette packets and glasses, she burst into tears and, crying repeatedly, "Oh dear, oh dear," tried to pick them up before running off stage, locking herself in her dressing room and attempting suicide.[26] Such concerts were an excruciating disaster, but in a sense also the performances of her career. *That* is how a legend behaves, cracking up before the whole world, abandoning every shred of "public" decency, being Judy Garland *sans complexe.*

From Jimi Hendrix, who died from sleeping tablets, to Brian

---

[25] Marc Bolan, "It's a Mad Life at the Top," *Daily Mirror*, November 28, 1972.
[26] Mickey Deans and Ann Pinchot, *Weep No More My Lady* (W. H. Allen, London, 1972).

Jones who had a fatal attack of asthma in his own swimming pool, from Gwili André, a Hollywood model who failed in films and died in a funeral pyre of her own press cuttings, to George Sanders who wrote that he was bored when he drugged himself to death, the victims of public life in the world of entertainment die as martyrs to the restless imperatives of their own being, which has become the cynosure of all eyes. Entertainment, from the most outrageous public copulation to the most boring situation comedy, is about private behavior *performed* in public for private citizens. The decline of the circus and the marching band is permanent and final.

Just as the celebration of private behavior in the world of public entertainment has intensified in parallel with the development and proliferation of the image recording and transmitting equipment used to portray it, so too is the disintegration of human social relationships that we have catalogued paralleled by a corresponding development in personalized equipment. Appliances as seemingly diverse as home video systems and electric dildoes facilitate the devolution of human sexual relationships into complex masturbatory fantasies as surely as the coming of safe contraception and do-it-yourself abortion are already beginning to remove the old corollaries of obligation and commitment from the traditional pattern of sexual union.

The private citizen is now able to survive the rootless, terrorized environment in which he lives in direct proportion to his or her ability to renounce any feelings of responsibility or concern for others. The pattern of media personalization, aided by the decline of live performance and the harassment of public broadcasting by censorship, clearly contributes to this process. The progression from national radio to local radio to underground radio to underground recording merely illustrates the widening scope of the trend that allowed the public cinema to give way to the private television receiver,[27] the massive

---

[27] For the price of one cinema ticket a TV set can be rented for a week.

hi-fi sound system to revert to noiseless headphones, the car radio to become merely the advance guard of a whole range of in-car entertainments—few of which are any longer dependent on centralized broadcasting control.

Attempts to resist by censorship the violent, erotic and antisocial image that a violent, erotic and antisocial society presents on its own cinema and television screens will prove—like the range of "treatments" continually applied to the ailing notion of community—to be counter-productive in the end. To ban sex and violence in the cinema and to resort to local censorship may well kill off the rump of the mass cinema audience—the majority of whom have already left for TV—but it cannot remove the erotic and violent fantasies from the minds of the workers, housewives, teenagers and businessmen who once made up that audience. Censorship of public spectacle merely *coincides* with the growth of home movies, blue movies, underground movies, Polaroid orgies and a hundred other forms of private indulgence, just as the banning of open soliciting and licensed prostitution in the present century *coincided* with the liberation of sex. The technology of the recorded image possesses the infinite ingenuity of the human being himself. Nothing can prevent the camera—the eye of the self who is another—from accompanying the privatized individual into the last unexplored fastnesses of his own being.

All this evidence of the close correspondence between the technical evolution of visual media equipment and the rapid privatization of consumer societies, like the interpretation of the social purpose of other consumer durables offered in an earlier chapter, does no more than confirm tendencies which are obvious at a larger scale. In the present century military conscription has introduced successive generations to the evasions and deceptions by which a crucial measure of freedom is maintained under an authoritarian regime. Popular motoring has accustomed millions to the reality of infringing the law two or three times a day. Drug taking has confirmed a pattern of private indulgence in the face of punitive attempts at prevention. Popular photography, cheap color reproduction and the cinema have converted millions to an image-based, voyeuristic form of sexuality. All these expressions of private freedom, irrespective of their legality, are part of the widespread and unremarkable social experience of the citizens of the consumer societies of the West, which is no different in any way from the legally approved forms of private pleasure associated with consumption in any society of private wealth. When governments discriminate between legal and illegal forms of pleasure and fantasy indulgence according to arbitrary notions derived from misunderstandings about the nature of their own societies, they face only failure. The arbitrary prohibition of some forms of nirvana at the expense of others, far from arresting the process of community decline, merely exacerbates it by creating instrumentally politicized patterns of resistance which in turn further depopulate the public realm by generating repression in the form of environmental terrorism. The process of privatization is irreversible in the present circumstances of the Western world, and the allegiance of its peoples to the dreams so indiscriminately displayed within it will survive any effort at reversal short of total destruction.

It will survive the reduction of the social contract to the uneasy spectacle of army, police and security forces making a vacant public realm "safe" for a population of drunken drivers, shoplifters, pot smokers, thieves, abortionists, fornicators and looters. It will survive the conversion of air travel into temporary imprisonment and the reduction of democracy to video-taped propaganda. It will survive the disintegration of mutual obligation and social community, the dissolution of the family, marriage and romantic love. It will survive everything that appears to threaten it because through the wreckage of its collapsed ideals, corrupted aims and lost opportunities its subjects know that this almost-achieved dream represents the dead center of the aspirations of the whole world. This is it. There is nothing else that is not worse.

Alone in a centrally heated, air-conditioned capsule, drugged, fed with music and erotic imagery, the parts of his consciousness separated into components that reach everywhere and nowhere, the private citizen of the future will have become one with the end of effort and the triumph of sensation divorced from action. When the barbarians arrive they will find him, like some ancient Greek sage, lost in contemplation, terrified and yet fearless, *listening* to himself.

Index

ABOUT THE AUTHOR

MARTIN PAWLEY was a practicing architect in England from 1962 to 1966, when he became the editor of *Architect's Journal*. He is currently a free-lance writer and journalist whose major publications include *Architecture versus Housing, Masters of Modern Architecture Series,* and frequent articles in *Architect's Journal, Design,* and *Architectural Design.* During 1972–1973 he was on a one-year grant at Cornell University in the Department of Architecture.